What People are Saying about

"Timely, useful, practical, realistic, readable!"
Richard D. Lamm, former Colorado Governor

"For anyone with aging parents or other loved ones, this is a must read. Simple, down to earth tips on how to deal with the inevitable."
Ernie Bjorkman, News Anchor, KWGN/Denver

"No matter how well you think you have your plans in place regarding the passing of a loved one, here you will find some helpful new information. If you have not yet begun to consider issues surrounding death, then you will definitely benefit from the advice in Jo Myers' book, given in a friendly, positive manner."
Jim White, Volunteers of America

"Laugh? I thought I'd die. And if I did, Jo Myers' fact- and fun-filled look at dealing with the inevitable would pull my family through."
Dick Kreck, former *Denver Post* Newspaper Columnist
Author of *Murder at the Brown Palace*

"Jo Myers has included a nice mix of heartfelt stories from her own experiences and valuable information on what you might expect before and after the big event. *Good to Go* made me wonder if I leave my body to science, will it become the corpse at which everyone snickers? Which of my siblings will become the leader and which will become Howard Hughes? Can I be the first to go so I don't have to deal with anyone else's leftover mess? Read it before it's too late."
LuAnn Buckstein, Comedienne
Chicken Lips and *Plastered in Paris* Comedy Groups

"Being adult children of parents in their 80s, we found *Good to Go* helpful and educational. Not only does Jo Myers introduce possibilities and concepts we never imagined, she provides answers, resources, and appropriate humor."
Murphy Huston, KOSI/Denver, and wife, Carol Huston, Teacher

"Thank you, Jo, for taking the time to write this valuable book. It has inspired me to pre-plan for my own end-of-life journey. The insights and lessons provided in *Good to Go* will help prepare me to love and give more of myself to my friends and family up until my death—and beyond."

Ruth A. Graham, Acupuncturist and Business Owner
Ancient Art Healing Center

"Jo Myers has written an impressive book. Her writing style is clear, dynamic, slightly breezy, personal (but not too), and so easy to read that it took me a while to fathom what a huge amount of information is included in *Good to Go*. I wish that a book like this had been given to me forty-five years ago when I learned that my mother was terminally ill with cancer. It still hurts to know that I didn't give her the sensitive, loving, emotional attention she must have so desperately craved."

Malcolm G. Stevenson, Technical Writer, retired

"Eventually, everyone has to deal with death. *Good to Go* struck a chord with me. After my grandmother died, we found she'd stocked up on 15 pounds of butter and more than 19 bottles of detergent. Jo's book will help you cope with the oddities surrounding the passing of loved ones and help you retain at least a portion of your sanity when surviving family members do something inappropriate. Read this book and realize you are not alone."

Angie Austin, Weather Anchor, KWGN/Denver

"An easy and straightforward read, *Good to Go* informs us what to expect when dealing with the passing of a loved one. This true-to-life story is a good reminder of possible circumstances anyone may face when a parent is dying. The lessons learned from the trials of Jo's family and friends could help make the experiences of others go much smoother."

Neysa Lettin, Teacher and Hospice Volunteer

"Jo Myers has used her bold, fun, and discerning style to create a wonderfully welcome place for the subject of death to land. I wanted to know more and more about the people involved and what I could learn from their experiences!"

Jenifer Madson, Financial Success Coach
Author of *A Financial Minute*

"Jo Myers has made light of, and cast light on, a subject of which hardly anyone will speak. *Good to Go* is an easy, insightful, and entertaining book that helps all of us come to terms with a relevant topic that was formerly taboo."

Dan Wiley, Actor, Comedian,
2003 Winner of *Laugh Across America*

"In her book, Jo Myers exhibits a deeper dimension than what listeners could know from her radio persona alone. *Good to Go* details, honestly and intimately, the impact of losing one's elders. Equally important, it is a practical tool with suggestions for dealing with funerals, legal issues, inheritance, the potential for disagreements—even estrangement from siblings and their spouses. The book shines with worthy advice and personal testimony."

Jean Galloway, President, The Galloway Group

"What a blessing to have this book as a guide during one's grief. I wish I could have read it before I lost my father to Alzheimer's and my mother to cancer. I found *Good to Go* to be not only comforting and therapeutic, but a real eye opener!"

Mike Nelson, Chief Meteorologist, KMGH/Denver
Author of *The Colorado Weather Book*

"Only Jo Myers could figure out how to make preparation for death funny. *Good to Go* amused me so that I read three-fourths of the book before it hit me. I am not good to go!"

George Johns, Broadcast Programmer, Consultant, Talent Coach

"Not just baby boomers, but everyone will benefit from this ultimate planning guide as we all must cope with the issues of death and dying. The author handles this sometimes-difficult topic with understanding and a happy dose of humor and lightness."

Herb Bowman, Director of Older Adult Ministries
United Methodist Church

"Jo has a way of taking her life experiences, bottling them up in a beautifully orchestrated lyric, and sharing them with others. Everyone will be affected by death in some way. Preparation and education early on will only make transition easier. *Good to Go* brings the point home."

Leslie Gail, Life Coach and Owner of New Life Focus Coaching

"For a generation that prides itself on the 'we can do anything' attitude . . . we've hesitated thinking about how we are going to 'do' our exit from this wild ride of life, let alone how we might help our parents and kids make *their* exits. This book is full of stories, tips, and practical advice on just that. But you will also howl, snicker, and outright laugh at a subject that none of us wants to think about. How about that? Another Baby Boomer making life and death just that much easier."

Rob "Sunny" Roseman, Meteorologist, KWGN/Denver,
Author of *Life's Little Ahas, Things I Wish I'd Known*

Good to Go

The ABCs of Death and Dying

The Ultimate Planning Guide

FOR BABY BOOMERS AND THEIR PARENTS

Jo Myers

Good to Go Publishing, LLC

Good to Go: The ABCs of Death and Dying
The Ultimate Planning Guide for Baby Boomers and Their Parents
by Jo Myers

ISBN Number 13: 978-0-9798178-0-9

Library of Congress Control Number: 2007903728

First Edition: August, 2007

Cover and Book design: Nick Zelinger, www.nzgraphics.com

Author photo by Ann E. Martin

Published by Good to Go Publishing, LLC

Visit our web site at www.goodtogothebook.com

Printed in the United States of America

The instructions and advice in this book are not intended as a substitute for legal advice, psychological counseling, or medical advice. The author and publisher disclaim any responsibility or liability resulting from actions advocated or discussed in this book. Those desiring or needing legal advice, medical advice, and/or counseling are encouraged to seek the services of competent professionals in those areas of expertise.

for
my parents
my aunt
and
my friend

TABLE OF CONTENTS

Introduction

"THAT WON'T HAPPEN in my family!"

I said that.

Who would have foreseen the day when my siblings and I would not get along with each other? Nobody . . . until our last parent died.

The stories in this book are about my family and the elders closest to me. (Some names have been changed.) They alert the reader to problems that may arise when parents, other relatives, and friends pass away. Expert advice and opinions are provided to help solve or avoid those problems. Get valuable information in this book from a funeral director, police officer, therapist, jeweler, veterinarian, hospice-care representative, estate sale company owner, financial planner, lawyer, real estate agent, caregiving executive, nurse, banker, obituary writer, and intuitive counselor. Learn about the amazing things emergency responders do. Receive instruction on how to visit a family in mourning from the most qualified authority, a women's Sunday school class.

Survivors have a better chance at a happy ending if parents make their wishes known, if they meet with family members as a tight-knit unit, if they have exit plans, and if they leave simple written instructions—even if the instructions are scribbled on a cocktail napkin!

Middle-aged offspring may act like children when Mommy and Daddy leave them alone . . . together . . . unsupervised. In my head, I hear my own father threaten from his grave, "You're never too old for a spanking!"

People may change when a loved one dies. Sometimes the change is for the better. Too often the change is for the worse, and irreparable damage is done. I have seen my own family fall from grace after the passing of my parents. I have dropped the ball myself in the relationships with my sisters and brother.

I have also witnessed—up close and personal through a dear friend's passing—the value of a good pre-plan and how other families often struggle and make mistakes, too.

This book contains helpful hints about preparation for one's own death or the death of another. Death happens. A good plan helps it happen with fairness, dignity, and integrity.

Jo Myers
Spring, 2007

Accidents Happen

A Is For Attitude

Affluent Aunt With Alzheimer's

A Is For Attitude Again

WHAT SHOULD HAVE killed Dad didn't.

The Big Accident happened after Mother died, when Dad was 76. After running errands, he stopped his truck at the end of the driveway to get the mail. He put the vehicle in park and stepped out. The truck malfunctioned—popped out of gear—and idled backward. And by *idled*, I don't mean *moseyed*. The truck was *moving*. Daycare kids played in its path in the yard across the street. He slipped trying to hop back in and the door knocked him down into the tight space underneath. The wheel rolled toward him between his legs. To avoid . . . um . . . . a worse injury, Dad curled over on his side. The wheel climbed up his leg and halted above his hip.

 First Responder Fact:

The low pressure pillow airbags used for extrication measure 24x24x2 inches. When used, the victim's vehicle is blocked with "cribbing" (small pieces of cut up wood), and the bag is set where the vehicle will be lifted. The bag is attached to an air bottle used on air packs called SCBAs (tanks worn on backs, similar to SCUBA tanks). Air bottles are pressured to 4500 psi (SCUBA tanks are pressured up to 600 psi). A regulator on the SCBA bottle reduces the pressure to 14 psi. The object (weighing up to 9 tons) is lifted and then stabilized, allowing people to be pulled out from under trucks or other entrapments.
Mike Osgood, Engineer/Firefighter

Emergency responders rushed to the rescue. With a giant, inflatable cushion, they lifted the truck, pulled Dad out, and got him in an ambulance, all within six minutes.

Of the offspring, I lived farthest away. Julie lived closest, thirty minutes away. Carolyn and Sammy lived within a few hours' drive. But Dad didn't normally require any assistance.

A suitcase in his hand, my husband, John, greeted me when I walked in the door at home. "There's been an accident. I've booked you a flight."

As he drove me to the airport, he said Dad was not expected to live. We discussed when John would join me with our boys for the funeral. I kissed him goodbye and got on the plane.

Dad's condition was listed as "critical." One look, and I knew it was worse than that. It was awful. His head was swollen, as if wasps had held a field day on it. Machines in ICU kept him alive.

A paramedic came by the waiting room to check on the status of the old man she had helped pull out from under a truck earlier that day.

"I thought for sure that guy was a goner," we heard her say. "His face was purple."

My sister and I introduced ourselves as the would-be goner's daughters. The paramedic detailed the accident and rescue, wished us luck, and moved on.

Dad was lucky. Miraculously, he survived. His knee was broken and his ribs were cracked, but the accident didn't kill him. Within a week, he was joking around, flirting with the nurses, and hallucinating from the painkillers.

All Doped Up And No Place To Go

 First Responders

often receive cards or letters from victims who let them know how they are doing. Regarding follow-up calls, *Denver area firefighter, Mike Osgood,* says, "We don't often do follow-up calls with the victims or victims' families. However, we do follow-ups with the hospital quite often. We call our hospital liaison or talk directly with the emergency room staff when we return with another patient. This does occur frequently with interesting or difficult cases."

I KEPT A diary of Dad's delusional outbursts.

"Look at that hamburger," he said as he pointed at the TV. "It's got mud all over it. What's that car doing parked outside my room?"

Outside his room on the second floor of a hospital? If I explained that he was seeing things because he was high on drugs, he argued with me. So, I humored him.

"Oh, they're just waiting to pick somebody up."

 A tip from Jo:

Journal the funny things said while a loved one is under the influence of painkillers. Read it to the person when he comes to. It might make the convalescence more enjoyable.

He narrowed his eyes in suspicion but seemed satisfied enough to not ask more questions about the car parked outside his room.

Dad talked in his sleep. In his dreams, he played college football and glided across a ballroom floor. He was happy to be alive, even if he did exist in an alternate universe.

It was a long recuperation.

Keeping Busy Helps

DAD NEVER DID completely get over getting run over by his truck, or "Christine," as we dubbed it. He joined a class action lawsuit against the manufacturer and received a settlement.

But no amount of money could ease the arthritis in his knees, which was exacerbated by the accident. This meant no more golf with his buddies, something he truly loved. Dad hobbled around with a cane for the rest of his life. It came in handy, though, as a prod for moving easily through crowds.

> ✔ **Legal Tip:**
>
> Only those in the judge's chamber are privy to information like how much money is awarded in a confidential settlement and everyone is sworn to secrecy, or the money could be taken away. "While that is true," says *Denver attorney, John N. McNamara, Jr.,* "terms of a settlement are usually structured so that the receiver is allowed to reveal the amount to his accountant, attorney, and spouse."

Nothing kept him away from the other activities he loved, including artwork, photography, and wood working. Dad's workshop hummed constantly with various projects. He helped build a fancy new senior center in his town and hauled prisoners back and forth from the county jail so the work could be done for free.

A family friend told him, "Sam, I'm just not comfortable with you driving prisoners around by yourself. That could be dangerous."

"Oh, now Jane, it's not that bad. The worst part is when I'm driving the van. It's not easy keeping a gun on those guys and both hands on the wheel at the same time."

Dad enjoyed trifling with the ladies.

The only trouble the prisoners actually gave my father was when they begged him to stop the van for a swimming break.

"Come on, sir. We wanna jump in the lake to cool off!"

But the answer was standard. "Now, ya'll boys know I can't let you do that."

Lessons Learned When Accidents Happen

- **You can survive** a serious accident at an advanced age.
- **Healing** is commensurate with attitude, activity, adaptation, and a sense of adventure.
- A patient's **determination** can speed the recovery process.
- **Humor** may help the healing.

A Is For Attitude

MOM DIDN'T SO much *die*. She faded and flickered out. No complaints. No drama.

Diabetes and heart disease took her away. As her health declined, she gave herself insulin shots, checked her own blood sugar, and regularly fell asleep at the kitchen table. Mom went through the motions of life—stuck in a wheelchair.

A physical therapist came over and asked her to squeeze a ball. Mother considered it nonsense. At times like these, her sense of humor clawed its way to the surface. She rolled her eyes and "pulled faces" when the therapist wasn't looking. After the therapist left for the day, Mom would throw the squeeze ball across the room, and it would land in a corner with a thud. It got a laugh out of me. But, nobody could make her enjoy therapy. It wasn't worth the hassle.

 Home Health Care Tip:

How do you motivate a person to participate in physical therapy? You need to be a very kind, encouraging drill sergeant-type personal trainer!
Audrey DiGiorgio, Administrator,
Continued Care Retirement Community

Tips For Home Health Care Attitude Adjustment

For the motivationally challenged person in need of physical therapy, try these tactics.

- **Encourage**, approach, re-approach, and re-re-approach.
- **Offer a reward in exchange for an effort**. Say something like, "How about 15 minutes on the exercise bike, and then we'll have coffee or tea together?"
- **Repeatedly remind the person about the benefits of effort** (walking on your own versus needing a wheelchair).
- **Consider whether pain medication needs to be taken** within a certain time frame before a therapy session.

Affluent Aunt With Alzheimer's

MOM'S SISTER, ADDY, was a childless widow who also had diabetes and Alzheimer's. She called everyone *sugar*, but pronounced it more like *shugah*, and she treated her nieces like the sweet substance she called us. She was always there for us, and we wanted to be there for her, too, as she aged, became ill, and began losing her faculties.

Because our cousin, Mary Beth, lived in the same area, she morphed from niece into niece *and* primary caregiver. Mary Beth's mother, another of Mom's sisters, had died years before. Mary Beth had cared for her before she died, so she had already gained extensive experience in caring for an aging loved one. Eventually, Addy had to be moved to a nursing home.

Aunt Addy was confused about many things and had forgotten many others. She thought her husband, Burke, was still alive—though he had been dead for 19 years—and often wondered aloud about what was taking him so long to return to the room. Sometimes she would tell visitors that he was down the hall talking to a man.

"I don't know what they're talking about for so long," she would mutter in frustration. Regaining her composure, Addy would then assure, "He should be back any minute. Wait right here because I know he'd like to see you."

Of course, Aunt Addy was not quite sure who we were, but she was always sure Burke would want to see us. Not recognizing her nieces did not inhibit her penchant for exchanging pleasantries. She liked visitors. Eventually she would ask, "Now, shugah, who do you belong to?"

It was common for Addy to confuse the television remote for the telephone. Once she handed it to my sister, Julie, saying, "It's for you." Julie humored her, put the remote up to her face—the channel numbers at her ear and the volume buttons at her lips—and engaged in an imaginary conversation. Addy told her she was talking too loud and asked her to please take the call outside the room. Julie complied and stepped into the hallway to complete her television remote control soliloquy.

It became obvious that Aunt Addy would never leave the nursing home. For this reason, her house had to be cleaned out and sold. Mary Beth took charge of the operation, and when Mary Beth put out the call to action, my sisters and I responded. We were able to jump in and help out in this way because my cousin and my sister, Julie, were appointed as co-powers of attorney for Aunt Addy.

Clearing out Aunt Addy's house became something of a treasure hunt. Her husband, Burke, had made his fortune working in the steel industry. As a child, I heard stories about Burke's offshore bank accounts and big game hunting trips to exotic places. Burke

> ✔ **Legal Tip:**
>
> If people can't make decisions for themselves, a designated power of attorney can. A personal or financial power of attorney is someone you trust who can make legal and financial decisions for you if you are unable to do so.
> *John N. McNamara, Jr.,*
> *Denver Attorney*

had been famous for showing off his money belt with its secret compartment on the inside of the strap. There, he tucked away gold kruggerands and large denominations of U.S. currency.

There were secret stashes of money, guns, and valuables scattered about Addy's home and yard. While she had once remembered the hiding places, Addy's recall ability was warped by Alzheimer's. Her recollections were foggy, at best. This made the chore of cleaning out her home more like an adventure. It was known that Uncle Burke had duct taped bags of money inside false pipes in the basement and had buried booty in the backyard. He even had a "panic room" installed in the house. This was a faux closet, complete with telephone, in which he and Addy could hide should intruders ever come looking for loot. Addy had once used the panic room to wait out a tornado. Because panic rooms are built to be secret rooms, we wondered what would have happened if Addy had wandered into that room and experienced a health problem while there. Would she have been found? Aunt Addy could probably have added more detail to what we already knew about her tricked-out house if Alzheimer's had not taken away her memories.

About The Alzheimer's Patient

- **Reach out.** Stay in touch. Even though your aunt, parent, or friend with Alzheimer's may not remember talking with you the minute she hangs up, try to keep in mind that she really enjoys the conversation, laughter, and shared moments as they happen. Do not give up on her just because it may be sad for *you* that she does not remember.

- **Keep the patient comfortable physically *and* mentally.** Imagine how it would feel to know that, at any moment, your mind could slip. Treat the patient with consideration.

- **Be patient** with the Alzheimer's patient. If she tells you the same story over and over, resist the urge to correct or point out that you have already heard the story. Behave as if you are hearing the story for the first time each time she tells it to you.

- Within reason and within the boundaries of safety, **allow the person with Alzheimer's to do what she wants to do.** If it gives joy, let it happen—even *help* it to happen.

- If driving is no longer an option, it is easy for the Alzheimer's patient to become housebound. **Look for safe ways to get this person out of the house.** To lunch, to the library, to a museum, or for a walk.

- **Laminate a copy of the patient's driver's license or other identification.** Put it on a lanyard to wear in case she wanders off.

- **It is especially important for a person diagnosed with Alzheimer's to designate a power of attorney** before losing her faculties.

- **Speaking of a power of attorney . . .** It is confusing but keep in mind that a person cannot be named a power of attorney without being appointed in a legal document also called a Power of Attorney. (I told you it was confusing.) The issues regarding power of attorney vary from state to state. These are the basics:
  - ✓ Someone delegated to hold **financial power of attorney** makes decisions for you about money matters if you are unable to make them yourself.

✓ A person given **health care power of attorney** makes medical decisions for you, if you are unable to do so yourself (relating to things like hospitals, nursing homes, and medical treatment options).

✓ Power of attorney is not automatically granted to next-of-kin. **If proper documents naming a power of attorney** are not in place prior to the need for it, the process to be named a power of attorney can drag through the court and be costly.

✓ Everyone **18 and older** should designate someone they trust to hold power of attorney.

✓ A power of attorney is immediately **null and void upon the death** of the individual who granted the right. At that time, only a designated Personal Representative (PR) is able to act on behalf of the deceased. In most cases, the PR has to be named or appointed by the Probate Court. **If you want to name someone to be a PR, put it in a Will.** Just be sure to give adequate thought to who that might be. You want someone with integrity who will look out for your best interests.

A Is For Attitude Again

MY FRIEND RUTH was dying. There were many people she could trust but she didn't trust many people. Ruthie and I first met when I rented the house across the street from her, and although we had been good friends for twenty-two years, she didn't trust me. I was determined to change that.

Taking Care Of Others

WHEN I MET my eccentric interior decorator neighbor, Ruthie, she was tethered to her 94-year-old mother, Maude. Maude had dementia, senility, or . . . something.

Ruthie explained, "It's like the record player works, only there's no needle in the tone arm."

Ruthie took outstanding care of her mom. She gave her a dolly, walked her, made sure she ate, and kept her in dry diapers. Neighbors and friends sometimes sat with Maude so Ruthie could go to yard sales (excellent sources of decorative items for her business), run an errand, or find a secondhand divan for a client. She had hired help in the way of Charlotte, who became as much a friend as an employee. A common sight was the three of them taking off in Ruthie's ragtop Cadillac, "The Gray Whale." It went up in flames one night, compliments of a Molotov cocktail.

"Who torched the Caddy?"

Ruthie said she had her ideas about that.

———

Mother Ruth, as she liked to call herself, was there for her neighbors, too. Soon after my first son, Beau, was born, his dad and I had an argument, which ended when he pushed me out onto the porch and locked the door. There I was, barefoot with the baby in my arms. My only option was to pad gingerly across the street and spend the night at Ruthie's house.

She greeted me with, "You look like 'Rastus Hades!' What's going on?"

She gave me the courage to get a divorce, eventually. Her advice was, "Sometimes you just have to kiss it, bless it, and let it go."

Ruth called me her "daughter by osmosis" and was like a grandmother to my sons. When we lived in Florida and my husband, John, was away on a long trip, she flew in for a couple of weeks. She cleaned up after a hurricane, got the boys off to school every morning, and taught my son, Beau, how to drive when he was only 14! Like some other spunky seniors I have known, Ruthie didn't give a thought to whether or not it was legal for Beau to drive. She had made the assessment of his readiness herself, and that was enough for her.

"Fourteen is old enough to drive a car!" she informed me, defensively, when I found out about their shenanigans. My car became high-centered on a fallen palm tree, and they needed a third person to rock it off. Otherwise, I might never have known.

A special bond developed between Beau and Ruth—but not between Ruth and my younger son, Jack, whom she regarded as "a smart aleck" ever since the morning she made breakfast, and he said he wasn't hungry. Ruthie called them "Darling Beau" and "That Jack."

 Police Blotter:

It is illegal for an unlicensed driver to operate a vehicle on public roads. If the car's owner allows this to occur, then the owner could be civilly and even criminally liable. If someone else is aware that a driver is too young for a license and allows it to occur, that someone else could be liable. Depending on what kind of additional conduct occurs under this permission, then there could be a charge of contributing to the delinquency of a minor. That charge can be a felony!
Captain Parris Bradley,
Criminal Investigations Commander

We moved back to Denver and saw Ruthie periodically, with special attention and time set aside for her for on Mother's Day, holidays, and in yard sale season.

The years went by in this way until Ruth got sick.

Jo's Thoughts About Friends And Neighbors

- **Trust takes time**, sometimes years, to develop.
- **Reciprocal relationships** work best. You do something for that person, and they do something for you (but not just for that reason!).
- **Neighbors** can become the best of friends. They can see you at your worst, in curlers, flappy bathrobe, and no makeup—and *still* take you in overnight.
- Some old people don't think twice about breaking a law. They seem to feel they've somehow **earned their *scofflaw* status,** paid for it with time "put in."

What I Learned From All My "A"s (That Hasn't Already Been Said)

- **Just as people live differently, they die differently,** and the elders closest to me were no exception.
  - ✓ One died relatively young after a long illness.
  - ✓ One died relatively old after a long illness.
  - ✓ One died because of an accident.
  - ✓ One died at home as planned.
- Through observing how they planned for the end of life, **I've learned that:**
  - ✓ Not having a plan is still a plan . . . but not a good plan.
  - ✓ The survivors' relationships change and not always for the best.
  - ✓ Wishes might not be honored after you are gone.

Bones Of Contention

The Handkerchiefs: Part I

AFTER MOTHER DIED and the rest of the family went home, I stayed with Dad for a week.

As I cleaned out Mom's things, I didn't toss out much. I mostly sorted through drawers and shelves and organized so Dad could find things after I left. Any gifts I had given Mom, I set aside for myself in a suitcase. Dad urged me to take some of Mother's other things, but I resisted the temptation.

My sister, Julie, called me and asked, "Where are Mother's handkerchiefs?"

"What handkerchiefs, Julie?"

She informed me that Mom's brother, Uncle Carl, had sent her a handkerchief as a birthday gift every year for many years. Julie wondered where they were.

"Didn't see any," I told her.

Mother owned a handkerchief? That was news to me. Preoccupied with the thoughtfulness of our uncle's yearly gesture to Mom, I didn't think to ask my sister if the handkerchiefs were important to her, Julie.

Later, I would discover that she sent her husband on a hankie hunt at the charity center. He rummaged through recent donations but didn't find any handkerchiefs. And I never gave them another thought until 11 years later, when Dad died.

The Handkerchiefs: Part II

IT WAS THE night of Dad's funeral.

My sisters, brother, and I found ourselves alone in Dad's art studio. I was planning to stay out the week for cleaning and said as much. My brother, Sam, said he was unable to do anything like that yet and would probably go home the next day. Julie asked me what I thought I was going to clean out.

I picked up an empty shoe box and snapped, "I thought I'd throw out this #!z%'n shoe box!"

My sister, Carolyn, said she didn't want anything done at the moment. She couldn't bear it. I pressed because I lived so far away, wanted to help out while I was there, and did not know when I would return.

Carolyn stated, "I don't want you staying, Jo. I don't want you cleaning out the house. You got to do that when Mother died, and I never got to go through her things."

I had stepped on some toes and didn't know it.

The realization came over me that I had, however inadvertently, hurt my siblings. Interestingly, while it appeared that I had hurt *them*, the fact that they had not told me hit *me* like a punch in the stomach. There had possibly been resentment toward me for a long time.

Words trickled from my mouth, "I was just doing what Dad wanted. I never thought . . ."

Julie mentioned something about Mom's handkerchiefs.

 A Tip From Jo:

Resolution is possible when communication is open! My sister has since taken responsibility for this complaint. She has admitted she knew I was there at the time of our mother's death, sorting through our mother's things, and that she could have helped but chose not to at the time.

 Therapist's Tip:

Humor will not solve relationship problems. However, it will do the following:

1. Allow the person who has just experienced being shut out to keep their thoughts and feelings moving and in touch; rather than shut down and move to rage and

2. Allow a person to feel supported until he or she can go back and deal with the original situation. Treating serious situations with humor can be cathartic. Use it when there is no way in the moment to deal with the relationships. Humor can get you through the difficult moments until there is an opportunity for individuals to meet privately to resolve their differences.

Vickie Kearney, MA, LPC

"Oh, the handkerchiefs again. I told you I never threw away any handkerchiefs. And I never donated any handkerchiefs or even knew Mother possessed any. Is this still about the handkerchiefs?" I raised my voice to a fevered pitch. Yelling assured she could hear me from two feet away.

I stood up. Carolyn asked where I was going.

"For a walk."

"I'm going with you."

"Fine."

Only I wanted solitude. I hated myself better in private.

As we walked down the driveway and around the block, I whined about Julie still being on me about those damn hankies.

Carolyn got testy. "Jo, this is not about YOU!"

We parted ways at the end of the street. Carolyn went around one block, and I walked around another. When we met up again at the streetlight, we hugged and walked up the road together. Someone was standing on Dad's porch smoking a cigarette and watching us. Our brother.

We called out, "Sammy! You look like Mother with a moustache!"

Mom and Sammy had shared thick torsos and skinny legs, as well as the habit of smoking. My brother described his own appearance as looking "like I'm riding a chicken."

> **Therapist's Tip:**
>
> Depending on the skill level of the individuals, the family may need a therapist or a mediator to aide in the process of coming to an understanding of one another and an acceptance of each individual's reality.
> *Vickie Kearney, MA, LPC*

The evening progressed or *digressed*, actually. We all drank wine. My brother changed over to bourbon, a bad sign.

My most vivid memory of the night we buried our father was my drunken brother slurring the announcement that he was driving home while his wife held him down on the bed and told him he was going nowhere. He hugged Dad's military flag to his chest and cried himself to sleep. The only thing missing was his thumb in his mouth. Sammy was again a welcome source of amusement.

Even so, the relationships with my siblings had become strained and tested. The next day we bid awkward goodbyes, and my husband attempted to comfort me in the rental car on the way to the airport.

"Don't worry. You don't ever have to see those people again."

Those people? *My* people. That hurt more than I would ever have imagined.

You-Know-What: Part III

MANY MONTHS AFTER Dad's death, while helping prepare for the sale of the house, my brother's wife, Robin, pulled down an old shirt box from the recesses of a closet and looked inside. Neatly folded and stored for at least twelve years, right under our noses, were Mom's handkerchiefs. Robin showed Carolyn the handkerchiefs and Carolyn showed Julie, who promptly put them in her car.

Handkerchief story over.

Before The Bones Of Contention Are Buried

- Seems **there's always *something*** in every family, some seemingly innocuous item, that can cause a rift and come between the survivors.
- **The issue might not be the actual item.** It might represent deeper, unexplored matters of which neither party is aware.

Caregivers Have Feelings, Too

Cremation: Making An Ash Of Yourself

The Unlikely And Impatient Caregiver

DAD WAS MOM'S caregiver, and he was amazing. He learned and performed home dialysis!

 Home Health Care Tip:

Do-it-yourself dialysis? It can happen! For peritoneal dialysis, a junior-size dialysis machine is delivered to the patient's home. A nurse visits to train the caregiver on how to do it, what to watch for, what to do if the backup battery system is needed, and when to call the doctor or nurse. This way, a better understanding of the disease process is learned by both caregiver and patient, perhaps better than what they would learn at the hospital.

Karen Paschal, R.N.,
Home Health Care Agency Director

This delayed Mom spending her days at a renal center. She eventually did need to get treated at such a facility, but Dad's home care of her postponed that for quite some time. Among the advantages of providing the treatment at home was that, at home, the dialysis took place overnight as she slept.

Dad set up a "ren center" in the house and gave my sister a tough time as he taught her the machine's nuances. Julie was Dad's backup. With him, you always had to have a backup. The man was intense about taking care of our mother. He possessed vast mechanical knowledge but very little patience. What patience he did have was only with Mom.

Our father, who had never spent time in the kitchen except for eating or walking through it, became chief cook and bottle washer. It was Mom who had always done all the cooking. She excelled at baking. No wonder she became a diabetic. There had always been something homemade in the cupboard: apple fritters, a pecan pie, or donuts from her deep fryer. Mom even handpicked the berries that went into her baked goods. Correction. Mom and *I* picked the berries.

First thing on summer mornings, she'd take me, the first kid out of bed, to a farm and pay pennies for buckets of "You-Pick-Em" produce. The bees and I buzzed around in the hot sun that dried off the dew within minutes after sunrise. This struck me as crazy and inconvenient when berries could be bought at the store, but it was cheaper this way, and our family saved money at every opportunity. We were a family of six living on an income of one.

In a switch of life-long roles, Dad made the meals. When I saw what he was going through, trying to come up with food that Mom could and would eat, I hired a nutritionist to devise month-long plans of customized menus, easy recipes, and shopping lists. Dad never knew I paid for this service. He thought this woman was a friend.

I hated lying, particularly knowing that my father did not tolerate lies and deceit. The first time I told my father a lie, I was five. I told him our little fluffy eight-pound puppy pulled the hose around the corner of the house and knocked over a stack of storm windows, breaking them. Of course, I had actually done it. He whipped me with a belt. After that, I was careful not to get caught lying.

 Manipulation Tip From Jo:

How do you hire a nutritionist behind your dad's back? You call a university or hospital and speak to a nutritionist. Ask the nutritionist for the cost of a month's worth of meal plans, along with shopping lists, for a person with the disease in question. Send the money to the nutritionist and the meal plans to your dad.

So even though I had been raised to tell the truth—and made a practice of it with my father, at least when it was practicable—I lied about the meal plans. It helped him cope.

Cherish The Caregivers

- **Caregivers are often family members of the person being cared for.** It's tough trying to take care of a loved one while you simultaneously lead your own life.

- The two most important words of advice for caregivers who are family members are **accept help.** Family and friends want to do something—anything. Let them.

- Kindly **request of helpers that they not take up your time** in the process. Let them know you will not be able to visit with them when they come over.

- **Designate one person** to coordinate scheduling the acceptance of help.

- **A caregiver might be a neighbor**. "A sweet lady in her 90s lives next door, and she wants to maintain her independence," says Baby Boomer Kathleen. "Because Lillian's children don't live nearby, I spend a few hours every day at her house. We have tea together, and I 'fix her up' with dinner. There are places that prepare meals from monthly menus. I can either go in and put them together myself or have the meals prepared and pick them up frozen with heating instructions. Either way, I can prepare individual portions at home and take them over to Lillian. She loves the food and especially likes that she can design her own meals. But it's never my treat. Lillian always insists on paying." This is a good way to go if there are no special dietary requirements. Some of these places even deliver. Go online or look in the telephone directory under "Meal Preparation."

Cremation: Making An Ash Of Yourself

I WAS THERE with four other friends of Ruth when the cremation company took her body. We gathered around the two men with the gurney and the large bag. One of them said, "Some people aren't comfortable watching the removal. Would you ladies like to leave the room while we do this?"

Almost in unison we said, "No, no. We want to be here."

We watched Ruthie leave her house and us and discussed how gently the men handled Ruth and how considerate they were of us, even though we surely must have appeared to be "lady lookie-loos" (nosey women who cannot let anything happen without being a part of it).

We spent the rest of the afternoon tidying up the house—our friend's home, where she had died, only hours before. After an amazing, emotional, lovely, and exhausting day together, the five of us—all friends of Ruth—were now friends of each other. We closed up the house and left.

Because she never paid top dollar for anything, Ruth shopped around for the most affordable cremation service in town a few weeks before she died. She left money earmarked for the company she had selected, along with contact information. It made for an expedient cremation. When she was done with life, Ruthie wanted to leave in a hurry . . . and leave only a trace of herself behind, in ash form.

> **The body removal** process should be dignified, concise, professional, careful, and caring. I always explain what is happening and ask if those family members and friends who are present would like to help.
> *Rhett Buckley,*
> *Funeral Director/Mortician*

I did not think that Ruth would like her friends to hop in cars and caravan down to the crematorium to observe her making an ash of herself (in a manner of speaking), so I didn't suggest it. No one else suggested it, either. Some things and people are best remembered as they were, I suppose.

The last thing Ruthie had in mind was to take up space in a cemetery, not even a little space for her ashes and a marker. That was not in keeping with her intent to just "tiptoe away" when she died.

She often mused about the scattering of her ashes. She wanted them strewn to the wind on a specific mountain top by a particular person. No muss, no fuss. Just a private "scattering." Her trustee collected the ashes from the crematorium, most likely encased in a box about the size of a big-city telephone book and wrapped like a gift in white paper. Then he handed them over to the chosen and forever unnamed (because of the legal ramifications of ash scattering at a public location) scatterer, the person who honored Ruth's wishes and, we hope, offered her ashes to the four winds with as much dignity as possible—dignity combined, of course, with nonchalance, so as not to attract the attention of the authorities.

Crème de la Cremation

- **You can arrange for your cremation ahead of time.** "I'll be cremated," says Gary, a retired salesman. "It's all set up with the funeral home and cemetery. My ashes will be buried in the ground with a marker over them. The marker is already there. It shows my birth date with a blank for my, uh, expiration date! I've buried two wives and my mother, and I don't want my daughters to have to make those kinds of decisions or pay for them. I've taken care of everything, and that's a relief. Now, I can get on with my life."

- **Cemeteries have special places for cremated remains.** Some have benches, cored to hold urns. Some have paneled areas that hold urns. A headstone listing several names, but placed in an area without enough space for burial, could indicate a "column burial" of stacked urns, each holding the ashes of a person listed.

- **Cremations can be viewed.** In some religions it is required. Some restrictions apply. Viewing might be through a window or via closed circuit TV in a separate building.

- **Mortuaries sometimes pay a fee** to have an outside crematory perform the service of cremation.
- If you want to feel confident that the body will be handled with respect and that the remains received are those of your loved one, **make sure the crematorium passes the "Mother Rule."** If you wouldn't do it to your own mother, it's not done. There are two things you can look for in a crematorium to help you make that determination.
  - ✓ **A strict identification process**, meaning ashes are enclosed in a polyurethane bag with an identification "coin" inside— all delivered in a plastic box.
  - ✓ **Assurance** that the body will be handled in a dignified manner.
- Even though **it is illegal** (without permission), many people scatter ashes of loved ones in public places like national parks and bodies of water. As soon as I tell you that rangers or security guards will likely look the other way, you will get busted. (And watch out for that I.D. *coin* while scattering ashes. Ouch!)
- A person's **ashes may only be scattered on private property with permission.**
- Make an ash of yourself . . . in space. There are companies that will send cremated remains to another part of the universe. **A smidgeon of a loved one's ashes may get launched** into orbit, go to the moon, enter deep space, or just go to space and come back. Prices vary, depending on flights. A web search of "ashes in space" will get you there.

Donate Your Body To Science

I'VE DONATED MY body to science. The paperwork has been completed. My cadaver card, prominently displayed in my wallet, is laminated. Medical students may ponder my anal retentiveness along with my auxiliary nipple.

> **Cadaver Tip:**
>
> How do you donate your body to science? Call your state's Anatomical Board or search for "willed body programs" on the Internet. Request the forms, and the information will be sent to you. Fill out the forms, send them in, and put the ID card in your wallet. In some states, the facility will pick up the body and handle the documents, all at no charge.
> *Kate Torgler,*
> *Colorado State Anatomical Board*

You read that correctly. My auxiliary nipple. I have three. The third one may look like a tiny birthmark, but it has all the features of the other two, sensitivity and plumbing, if you know what I mean.

Lactation was painful with my first child. The second time, I was ready. I wrapped myself, like an Asian woman in ancient times might have bound her feet so they would stay small and contained. This discouraged the milk at that location. Thus, the third nipple retained its status as birthmark and caused me no more problems.

The doctor who discovered my "dis-growth of cells" (his words and nobody else's) was the man who had brought me into this world, our family doctor. When I was ten, my mother dragged me into his office and demanded he confirm I had an extra nipple. When the doctor proclaimed it to be a dis-growth of cells, my mother replied that she knew what he meant. I sat half dressed on the examination table and imagined life as a carnival sideshow freak.

Doctors have since had mixed reactions. Some claim to have never before seen an auxiliary nipple while others say they have seen more than three on a person. One stated that a woman he had examined had nipples "like a dog, with little ones running down both sides under the regular, symmetrical two breasts."

I figure future Ob-Gyns—and future mothers with more than the usual allotment of mammary glands—will benefit from studying my surfeit of nipples . . . uh, sometimes referred to by doctors as a *birth defect*. So I have promised myself to the Anatomical Board.

Another reason I have made the cadaver commitment? My husband and I are frugal. If you donate your body to science, cremation is free!

When you die, it goes something like this. Your survivors call the nice medical people and, in some states, they pick up the corpse. They do what they do with it. Then, a couple of years or so later, your body is cremated, and your survivors get a call from someone who tells them to pick up your ashes. In my state, survivors of the deceased are responsible for delivery of the cadaver.

Cadaver Travel Arrangements:
Call a local funeral director or a mortuary service provider. The Anatomical Board can make recommendations. You can pre-arrange (pre-pay with locked-in prices), which means that, upon the death of a body donor, two quick phone calls handle it all––one to the State Anatomical Board and one to the pre-arranged mortuary for transport.
Kate Torgler,
Colorado State Anatomical Board

The Hidden Cost Of Body Donation,
(depending on where you live, or die): Anatomical Boards do not always pick up bodies or do the paperwork. Body removal and transport can cost hundreds of dollars. Outside of a certain radius, there is likely an additional per-mile charge. If the death occurs out of state, the body donation might be transferable. If not, the cost of a flight and body container would apply with additional charges for driving the body to and from airports. Expect to pay $400 to $800 for body transportation services and any refrigeration that might be needed. This charge includes doing the paperwork (the handling and signing of documents and certificates). Families can do all this, but it's time-consuming and can be stressful, an enormous inconvenience during a time of grief.
Rhett Buckley,
Funeral Director/Mortician

While it might be legal to pile a body into your car and ride in the local HOV lane (although a cop could give you a ticket if it's just the "two" of you), it is not legal to transport a body across the state line. Minimally, a burial-transit permit is required to do this. An ambulance service might be able to get my body where it needs to go, for a price. My husband or sons will likely have to pay for the transport of my corpse—which they may see as one final gift to me or, just as likely, will view as one final expense racked up by Jo.

"Mom, Stop Talking."

ONE SON SAID he didn't care what I did with my body and didn't want to think about it. The other son protested when he learned I had donated myself to science.

"I don't know if I'm comfortable with that, Mom."

He was unimpressed that I might end up a crash-test dummy instead of a surgical guinea pig. Cadavers don't have voices. They end up where they're needed.

> **Donation Information:**
> Bodies that are donated to science are treated with the utmost respect. Medical students are reminded that each cadaver represents a parent, a teacher, a civil servant, a coach. Students are given the opportunity to communicate with the family members of the deceased, often by writing a letter of gratitude. The bodies are draped at all times, and only those areas that are under investigation are uncovered. The gift of donation is very much appreciated by all in health care.
> *Bridget Dunn, MD, Teaching Physician*

Destination Donation

- I am re-thinking my wishes and wondering if they will even be honored, anyway. **A hassle in the midst of grief could cause a wish to be ignored.** If I want something done when I die, I had better do my best to arrange it beforehand and get my family to agree. (I know, I know. After I'm gone they can change their minds . . . and even revise history by altering their memories of my wishes.)

- *If I die in a flaming car wreck* (a trademark phrase of mine used to remind my kids that I won't always be here to kick around), will my family pick up the pieces? Actually, there is no need for such gruesome imagery because they will not need to pick up any pieces if I die in a car wreck. The Anatomical Board **cannot accept a body** if any of the following happen.

✓ Death is caused by an accident or trauma.

✓ Organs have been removed for transplant at the time of death (except the eyes).

✓ The deceased had major surgery thirty days prior to death.

✓ The body has deteriorated.

✓ The deceased had a dangerous, contagious disease at the time of death.

✓ The body is emaciated or obese.

- Acceptability can be determined **only at the time of death.**

- In addition to the State Anatomical Board, **there are private companies that accept body donations** for medical study, and some even absorb the cost for transport or other things. Do a web search of "body donation", and you will learn more.

- If you do not want to go the "full-body" route but still want to do something nice for someone else, posthumously, **be an organ/tissue donor** (web search those words for more information). Laws and registration procedures vary from state to state, but basically, you indicate on your driver's license that you are a donor and register with your state's organization, and (you are about to read something very important) **TELL YOUR FAMILY ABOUT IT IMMEDIATELY.** When you die, time will be of the essence for transplantation to occur. Nobody wants to wait around while your family members argue over whether to give away your body parts. The waiting time for donated organs is already painfully long.

- You can **donate your brain** (brain *tissue*, actually) **to a brain bank**, so that scientists and medical doctors may learn more about what makes it tick. Go online to make it happen. Suggested web search words include "brain tissue donation."
- Urban legends and myths about body and body part donation have caused massive recoil at times, but **the truth is powerful stuff.** Your death may help someone else live. Your death may help a scientist, doctor, nurse, emergency responder, safety expert, and others help others . . . help others . . . help others . . . help others . . . **Did I mention you would be helping others?**

Etiquette Of Sympathy And Grief

E Is For Eulogy

After Mom Died

MY SISTERS AND I divided up duties on the night of Mom's funeral, who would send thank-you notes for what and other tasks. We felt it was important to acknowledge the expressions of sympathy that had come our way, and we wanted to take care of the niceties for our father so he could just focus on grieving. Because we had never witnessed our brother even address an envelope, we were not certain he had ever written a thank-you note. We assigned him the task of hanging out with Dad to provide distraction, participate in male bonding rituals like drinking beer, and otherwise take care of the guy stuff.

Thank-you notes were sent to everyone who signed the visitation guest register at the funeral home. A special note went to the family friend who hugged my neck and consoled, "There's nothing like losing your momma." No truer words were ever spoken, as Mom liked to say.

Thank-you notes also went to funeral attendees, those who sent flowers, those who called with their sympathies, and the many people who had brought food. The preacher who conducted Mom's funeral service received a thank-you note with a check in it, even though he had not charged us. We thought it was the right thing to do.

My sister, Carolyn, wrote a letter to those people in Mom's address book we didn't see or talk to right after Mom died. She explained the illness that had led to Mother's death, what good care Dad had given her, and assured each one that Mom had enjoyed having them in her life.

One of Mother's high school friends, whom we had called to tell of Mother's passing, sent us a stack of photos from their teen-age years in the 1930s. For that, the lady received a thank-you note *and* a permanent spot on my Christmas card list.

Many people had stopped by the house to share their remembrances of Mom, and they all received thank-you notes. One neighbor re-told a story I had heard many times about Mom terrorizing the neighborhood one Halloween. She had dressed in a clown suit, paired up with another woman, and went out trick or treating—late, after the children had made their rounds.

"Well, your momma put on a mask and a wig so I wouldn't know who she was, and she banged on my door. When I opened the door, she was holding a cigarette and said 'trick or treat' in a gruff voice. I said, 'Young man, if you're old enough to smoke, you're too old to trick or treat.' That's when she grabbed at the bowl of candy and pulled on it. We were fightin' over the bowl—'cuz neither one was gonna let go—and old Eileen Wetzel jumped out of the bushes wavin' a flashlight and laughin' her head off. That's when I realized I'd been had. Your momma about scared me half to death!"

 A Tip From Jo:

Mind Your Manners.

"They" (those anonymous authorities on everything) say thank-you notes should be sent to anyone who:

- Calls on the phone.
- Visits the house.
- Attends the funeral.
- Makes a donation in the deceased's name.
- Sends flowers.

Hearing that story again brought my mother back to life, if only for a moment. The storyteller got an extra-special thank-you note from me.

I was sticking around for a few days, so I volunteered to perform the service of returning dishes to friends and neighbors who had brought food to the house. We had barely touched any of it, because no one had an appetite, but there were platters, bowls, and Tupperware to return—and appreciation to extend for their efforts.

After Dad Died

JUST AS WE had done when Mother died, we pulled out Dad's address book when he died and called everyone he knew. One man, who now lived in Arizona, inquired about a ring he had made for my father. I knew the ring immediately as he described it, because Dad wore it all the time. It had turquoise and other precious stones set in silver. We told him the ring was prized by the family and would be passed on to Dad's son, Sammy. He asked for the addresses of all of the girls and, to our surprise, each of us later received a ring, fashioned by Dad's friend. It was a beautiful remembrance of Dad.

People lined up around the outside of the funeral home for visitation when Dad died. With every person who came by to honor my dad, I cried a little bit more. A family friend gave me his handkerchief. A couple of weeks later, I sent him a new Irish linen handkerchief with a note thanking him for his thoughtfulness.

Therapist's Tip:

Remembering those who help ease grief can be therapeutic. Look for ways to do this as well as helping others with the grieving process.
Vickie Kearney, MA, LPC

Following the funeral, a short graveside ceremony was held, during which my brother received Dad's triangularly folded, military-service-earned American flag. There is a long history of funeral etiquette where veterans are concerned, and this tradition was honored at Dad's funeral.

Dad had been a crew chief in the Army Air Corp, stationed in Europe during World War II. During the war, when he wasn't in the air—standing on a flak jacket between the pilots of a cargo plane, supervising troops—he was on the ground, painting voluptuous women on the sides of airplanes.

My brother, my sisters, and I actually did not know he was a WWII airplane artist until an old military buddy sent him photos before he died.

"Who painted this plane, Dad?

"Oh, I did that. I painted a couple of those."

We were proud to know that our father had been an airman and an artist during the war. We were grateful to have the photos, especially after he died.

While we were at the funeral, a representative from Dad's Sunday school class house-sat for us, giving us the peace of mind of knowing the house would not be targeted by a burglar during the funeral—unfortunately not an uncommon occurrence.

After the interment, we grabbed some of the flowers and returned home to nosh on potluck the rest of the day. Dad's Sunday school class, other friends, and neighbors had prepared a veritable feast.

Just as I did when Mom died, I took on the chore of returning the

 Planes from WWII and other eras:

There is a military airplane "graveyard," at Davis-Monthon Air Force Base, near Tucson, Arizona. Planes from WWII and other by-gone eras are parked there, and arrangements may be made to tour the site. Web search the words, "military airplane graveyard."
(If I find the planes my Dad painted there, I will write the base a nice thank-you note.)

dishes to those who had brought food for Dad's post-funeral get together. To my dismay, I found dishes at the house that had been left when Mom died more than a decade earlier. The names and dates were on curling masking tape, barely holding on. I had left before all the dishes could be returned back then, and Dad had promised to take care of it. I felt sheepish as I returned *those* platters, bowls, and Tupperware.

Etiquette Essentials

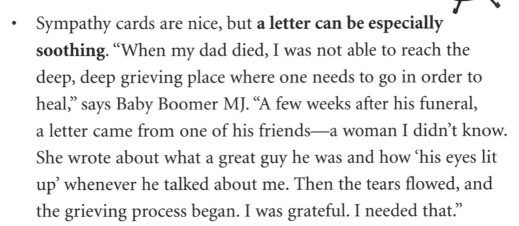

- Sympathy cards are nice, but **a letter can be especially soothing**. "When my dad died, I was not able to reach the deep, deep grieving place where one needs to go in order to heal," says Baby Boomer MJ. "A few weeks after his funeral, a letter came from one of his friends—a woman I didn't know. She wrote about what a great guy he was and how 'his eyes lit up' whenever he talked about me. Then the tears flowed, and the grieving process began. I was grateful. I needed that."
- **How to visit a family in mourning:**
  - ✓ **Only one person should deliver** the food to a family in mourning. Too many strangers coming and going is intrusive and causes confusion. Make sure the family is comfortable with the designated deliverer.
  - ✓ The representative should **take no more than 20 minutes** for delivery of food, instructions, and words of comfort.
  - ✓ **Ask the family to provide four or five choices of food** preferences. Frozen food works well because it can be heated when convenient.
  - ✓ Determine **how many days** of food care are needed and **how many people** will be present.

✓ Remember, **there could be a need for food BEFORE** as well as after the loved one has passed away.

✓ **Coffee and tissue**s are always welcome gifts!

• Another nice thing to do for a grieving family? Provide a person to house-sit during the visitation, funeral, and interment. **Burglars sometimes peruse the newspaper obituarie**s and figure out addresses. At the time of a service they can easily burglarize a home. If there is a car in the driveway and someone in the house, any such robbery is likely thwarted. Sadly, not only is the home of a dead person attractive to random thieves, but distant relatives have ransacked and stolen while the close family members are at the funeral or graveside service.

Tips for visiting a grieving family were provided by Kay Oppegaard, Rev. Ruth Pittenger, and Serendipity Sunday School Class, Littleton United Methodist Church in Colorado.

E Is For Eulogy

DAD, AN AVID churchgoer, wanted the eulogy for Mom delivered by the preacher from his church. The preacher did not know her, so a large part of her eulogy consisted of his reading aloud her newspaper obituary. There were typos and mispronounced words, but Dad did not seem to mind. In his grief, he might not have noticed.

In an effort to avoid a repeat of the impersonal memorialization of our mother, Carolyn and I wrote a large part of the eulogy for our father's service. Delivered by Dad's preacher, it was a letter of appreciation thanking Dad for being Mom's provider and diligent caregiver, a positive influence on us, and a helper in the community.

My aunt Addy's eulogy was delivered at the cemetery. It was a cold day. Her surviving friends were frail and few, so the graveside service was short and sweet.

There was no eulogy for my friend Ruth. She made us promise. But her inner circle of friends gathered for dinner, and we toasted the old girl. She would have been all right with that.

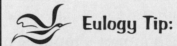 **Eulogy Tip:**

"I have the secret to writing a good eulogy," claims *David Friedli, Associate Pastor of Highland Park Church in Nashville, Tennessee.* "Do it before you die. If you don't, the person left to write it will put down whatever he or she wants. Most people try to 'eulogize the deceased into heaven' by telling how good they were and how long they attended church. They name all the organizations the person belonged to, but you hardly ever hear about their personality—what they were really like. If you want people to know who you were and what you thought, write your own eulogy and leave it for a designated person to deliver, to be read aloud at your memorial service."

Eulogy Do's And Don'ts

- The presenter should **know the deceased well** and be able to give the talk without crying too much. If you are designated to give the eulogy, practice it at least ten times to ensure that you can get through it without losing composure.
- **Make sure the eulogy is about the deceased.** The presenter should not use the eulogy to advance his or her own agenda.
- **How much money should be offered for a eulogy?** This payment is known as an "honorarium" and may be $150 to $200. A funeral home can provide a eulogist.
- If you write a eulogy, be sure to put in some pronunciation guides.
- **One formula for writing a Eulogy:** Baby Boomer Gary D. suggests you present it as a book review. "Give the decedent's life a title using a phrase, motto, or theme by which the person lived. Example: 'Living Large.' Give an overview in the 'foreword of the book,' by citing examples of why the title fits the person. Talk about how the deceased 'lived large' and, perhaps, detail your relationship with the deceased, how you knew him or her. Chapter One could be stories of the decedent's life with his or her partner. In Chapter Two, tell about the children and their relationship with the deceased. Chapter Three might be a wrap-up. Talk about friendships, talents, and any other attributes of the deceased."

Let's Put The Fun Back In Funeral

Kids Do The Darndest Things

THE SUN CAME out on the day of Mom's funeral. My 3-year-old, Jack, was antsy. I told Jack that as soon as we "put 'MeeMaw' in the ground" (explaining his grandmother's burial in understandable preschool terms), he could go outside and play.

As the memorial service dragged on, Jack couldn't take any more. He threw himself on the floor like a rag doll in front of Mother's casket, rolled around as if in need of an exorcism, and began "speaking in tongues."

He wailed for all to hear. "I want to put MeeMaw in the ground! I want to put MeeMaw in the ground! I want to put MeeMaw . . . IN . . . THE . . . GROUND!" Through a haze of mortification and grief, I racked my brain for a parenting technique that would quickly stop this impromptu, demonic possession-like behavior.

Then I heard laughter. Soon everyone was laughing, me included.

 A Tip From Jo:

Kids can provide great comic relief! But if you are concerned about how children might react to death and the ceremonies that surround it, consult a therapist or grief counselor. You might be interested to know that certain burial packages available through funeral homes offer a 24/7 toll-free hotline, staffed by counselors with advanced degrees, designed to help clients handle these types of concerns and work through grief. Ask about it when making funeral arrangements.

Mom did not attend church regularly, so we picked out songs that were not hymns as music for the ceremony. Someone jokingly suggested an old favorite of Mother's, *Don't Get Around Much Anymore. Ain't Misbehavin'* was another facetious proposal.

We howled with irreverent laughter. Mother would have laughed, too. She was the "Queen of Sarcasm" and loved a good joke, even if it was played on her.

With the exception of my little boy's animated caterwaul on the chapel carpet, it was not a memorable memorial to my mom.

Elderly Cousins Do The Darndest Things

YEARS LATER, DURING Dad's funeral service, Jack was a "dignified teenager" (talk about an oxymoron!) and refrained from making a scene. It was our octogenarian cousin, Richard, who stole the show when he hollered out from his wheelchair, "I'M GONNA NEED SOME HELP HERE," because he had to go to the bathroom.

Looks Aren't Everything

Secular Song Suggestions For Services:

There are probably as many choices as there are people, but here's a *Top Ten* of popular, secular selections for funerals:

1. *Somewhere Over the Rainbow*
2. *What A Wonderful World*
3. *Wind Beneath My Wings*
4. *Somewhere My Love (Lara's Theme)*
5. *Daddy's Hands*
6. *Imagine*
7. *(No) Tears in Heaven*
8. *You'll Never Walk Alone*
9. *My Heart Will Go On* from *Titanic*
10. *I Will Remember You*

Song list courtesy of
Andrea Tabler,
Funeral Music Provider

FOR THE VISITATION, Dad's casket was open. This was despite big stitches running across his head like a creation of Dr. Frankenstein (no offense to Dad's surgeon). Dad had many close friends, and closure was important for them, too. These people expected to see him when they said goodbye. He looked awful but would not have cared.

"What does it matter how I look?" he would have said. "I'm not going to a beauty pageant!"

Open Casket Commentary:

"Family and friends don't have to be denied a comforting, lasting image of a loved one," says *Mike Hawkins, Funeral Director.* "As a mortician trained in extensive restoration technique that includes the application of plastic surgery materials, I close lacerations with industry glue and use surface materials—waxes—to completely obscure incisions. 'Cosmetizing' from the inside of the body is done with carefully tinted embalming fluid, which, for example, replaces the natural rosiness of the skin."

Pallbearer duties fell on the young men of the family, who carried out their grandfather's casket and slid it in the hearse.

We got into cars lined up for the procession to the cemetery. Dad's girl-friend, Ellie, sat beside me. I welcomed the distraction of her friendly chatter.

"I guess they'll be calling me 'The Black Widow' now," Ellie mused.

"Beg pardon?"

"Well, your daddy died while he was going out with me. Another man died while we were dating. And my husband died. I might be bad luck."

A little gasp caught in my throat, but I choked it down with a smile. Dad had been in love with this woman, and she was a sweetheart to him. He never saw her as a bad luck charm, and neither did I.

Funeral Note:

If pallbearers are weak or elderly, a casket is placed on a lawn cart, which can be pushed or guided. That way, very little lifting or carrying is necessary. The funeral home and cemetery personnel are available for assistance when transferring the casket from the lawn cart to a lowering device.
Larry Tabler, Funeral Director

What Now?

MY FRIEND, RUTH, waved off a funeral. She emphatically did not want a memorial service. She was adamant about her reason. "I've walked behind too many hearses."

> **Fun Funeral Activity:**
> In New Orleans, we have what's called "The Second Line" behind the more somber "First Line," where a procession of people in party clothes march, dance, play instruments, and sing in celebration of the decedent's life.
> *Cory Smith, Jazz Funeral Coordinator, Thibodaux's Funeral Service, New Orleans*

Funeral Directions

- "It's one of the worst times of your life, and **you're supposed to be hosting a party.**" (Overheard at a visitation.)
- **Funerals are about** 1) Honoring the deceased person's wishes; 2) Celebrating the life of the deceased; and 3) Survivors coping with grief and relationships.
- **A traditional funeral with visitation can cost thousands of dollars** if complete services are included and all paperwork—everything from the doctor's signature to necessary filings—is handled. **The funeral home employees do the running around, so the family doesn't have to deal with it.**
- Burial plots usually range from $1,500 to $10,000, the price difference based on the type of plot and the location.
- The fewer people involved the better. Especially at the funeral home, **it is ideal for one person to make all the decisions.** (But how many family members are willing to let *that* happen?) One funeral director told me she has had to

"clear the room" to have a private conversation with the decision-maker of the family.

- **Let the funeral director be "The Heavy"** (in a nice way, of course!).
- Certain people may feel powerless and out of control when death occurs. Other **people try to take control, overstepping boundaries** in the process, even if they think they are helping their loved ones. If non-family members try to take over the process of making arrangements, and this is not acceptable to family members, a conversation with the funeral director should clarify that only family members may actually make decisions. However, do not expect a funeral director to play referee. He or she probably knows from experience that the family member or friend who "doesn't win" could become angry—and, therefore, *volatile*—and cause some real trouble.
- **Live music can liven things up.** A pianist, guitarist, or singer are good for indoor funeral services. Musicians like bagpipers or trumpet players (*Taps*) sound better outside. Unless the performer is a friend, fees usually apply.
- **Butterfly and dove releases** are available for graveside services. A funeral home can put you in touch with these providers.
- **Balloons** may not be suitable for outside services, because they can be unkind to the environment and dangerous to wildlife if ingested. (My husband says he wants his ashes poured into balloons and released into the air. We're having discussions about other options for his ashes.)
- **Speak to the funeral director about any idea** you might have for memorialization. It cannot hurt to run it up the flagpole, *literally*. For example, if the deceased was a sports fan, you

could request that the flag of his or her favorite team be flown at the cemetery on the day of the service. It has been done.

- **Police escorts** and hired security are other services to ponder.
- At the cemetery behind my home, I have seen a restored, **horse-drawn vintage funeral carriage** leading a procession. Such a vehicle might be available for hire where you live, too.
- Hand out pre-printed, stamped, and addressed **Memory Cards** at a funeral service. **Guests write down remembrances** of the deceased and send them back to the family for inclusion in a Memory Book.
- "I saved flowers from my mother's funeral service," says Baby Boomer Nancy. "I dried one arrangement for placement in a shadow box. Other flowers I pressed and framed. They look great on the walls of my bedroom." A florist can give advice for such projects.

From Beyond The Grave

AFTER MOTHER'S DEATH, I stayed an extra week to help Dad and keep him company. He asked if I would clean out Mom's closets and cart stuff off to the donation center, no small task. For more than forty years, my parents had thrown away little.

 A Question About Home Health Care:

Why do people abandon sick friends? For the elderly, sickness and death might be too close for comfort. Also, some people fear that a non-contagious disease can somehow be "caught."
Audrey DiGiorgio, Administrator, Continued Care Retirement Community

Dad requested that Mother's nicest clothes be delivered to her friend, Jenny, who was just about my mother's only friend at the end.

Mom loved getting out of the house, and Jenny made it happen. Mom didn't seem particularly happy to have visitors, anyway. It was too much effort to receive them.

Mom Says, "Hi"

WHILE GOING THROUGH Mom's purses, I found wadded-up tissues, golf score-cards, old tubes of lipstick, and—Hey, what's this?—a letter she had written years before . . . to me. The letter had been sealed, addressed, and forgotten. Holding my breath, I steadied myself on the edge of her bed and gently tore the letter open. She had written it before my children were born, right after Dad retired. She complained with good nature, that he was "under foot" and "driving her crazy." I heard her Southern alto voice in my head, and it was clear and beautiful, as if she was in the room.

Things Got Weird

A STRANGE THING happened a few days after Ruthie died. Someone mailed her sister, Margaret, photographs of Ruthie on her deathbed. Margaret was audibly upset when she called me. She described the pictures as ghoulish-looking and said they were enclosed in an envelope with no message and no name above the return address, which was given as Ruthie's address. A time and date were written on the backs of the pictures—10 p.m., the night before Ruthie died.

"Who would do such a thing?" Margaret asked me.

I had no answer.

Grave Consequences

"UNWANTED ANONYMOUS CONTACT made by mail, phone, text messaging, or by any other means, which is designed to harass or intimidate is known as harassment," cautions *Captain Parris Bradley, Criminal Investigations Commander.* "If it can be shown who did it, the conduct could be considered illegal and actionable. The jurisdiction for such an investigation is either from the venue where the message was sent, or where it was received, or both. There is an issue with First Amendment rights to free speech, but it is the anonymity aspect that may bring into play the criminal authorities."

Hospice

Oh, Nurse!

RUTH BECAME CONFUSED during her final months. As summer heated up, her confusion intensified. The cancer was taking its toll. A lot of time was spent keeping her dressings in place and trying to manage her pain. Ruth was afraid she would become addicted to the morphine, so she would wait until she was really hurting before taking a dose.

Plus, the drugs made her constipated.

Ruth was on the bed, rocking in pain, when I arrived one morning. I called the hospice nurse.

She asked if Ruth had any *Fleets*.

"Fleets?"

"Enemas."

I looked in the cabinets. Yes. No. The stuff was out-of-date by three years. I called the neighbor, Jim. He said he would buy some and drop them off. He must have meant that *literally*, because he practically threw them in the front door and sped away.

I called the hospice nurse again.

"I've got them."

"I'm on the other side of town with a patient. Could you give them to her?"

 Hospice Quote:

We frequently hear concerns expressed about possible addiction to pain medications. True addiction means the person would take the pain medication for any reason other than treating pain. This occurs *very rarely* in patients. Addiction is often confused with physical dependence, which can develop with many different medications. Physical dependence is not the same as addiction and does not cause addiction. If the person's pain decreases, they take less medication. If their pain stops, we teach them to decrease gradually and then stop the medication to avoid withdrawal symptoms resulting from physical dependence.
Linda Hudson, RN, BSN, CMT, CHPN, Nurse Educator, The Denver Hospice

 Hospice is friendly, holistic, low-tech, person-centered care. Hospice gives support to family and friends.
Jennifer Ballentine, Manager of Professional Programs, Colorado Hospice Organization

"Them?" I had three.

"Two. You've done this before?"

"Sure." But not to someone else, someone in such a state of suffering.

They don't call them "Fleets" for nothing.

The "fast-acting formula" gave her some relief, but she was still in a bad way and exhausted from the ordeal. By the time the hospice nurse arrived, Ruth was asleep after giving herself a dropper of morphine.

> **Hospice** care plans are individualized to meet specific needs of specific patients. Typically, nurses visit at least once a week or more often, if needed. CNAs (certified nursing assistants) may come as often as every day, but this is rare. CNAs usually visit two to three times a week. A patient may decline visits from any hospice team member (social worker, chaplain, CNA) except the nurse.
> *Jennifer Ballentine, Manager of Professional Programs, Colorado Hospice Organization*

> The bedrock of **Hospice** care is to maintain the patient's ability to make his or her own decisions. The challenge is keeping support for independence and control balanced with safety and comfort. Many in-home hospice patients reach a point when they need someone with them at all times to avoid falls, over or under medication, and see to personal care. If neither family member nor trusted friend is available, hospice can arrange for the person to be moved to a nursing home where the hospice team continues to provide care. Some hospices have dedicated inpatient residences for this level of care.
> *Jennifer Ballentine,*
> *Manager of Professional Programs,*
> *Colorado Hospice Organization*

The nurse examined her. "It looks like she's taken a fall. See her puffy lip? Did she fall?"

Not that I knew of.

To her patient, the nurse said, "Ruthie, did you fall down last night?"

"Her feet are swollen, too. Let's get them elevated," the nurse said to me.

Ruth was too out of it to say much. She had over-medicated herself. The nurse said it was likely she had fallen when no one else was there and didn't remember it or maybe didn't want to admit it, for fear of losing her independence.

The Last Day Together

THE MORNING RUTHIE died, her neighbor, Marie, stopped by to check on her and called me at work. "She's not going to last much longer. I'm thinking minutes."

I rushed over. When I walked in the door, Bella, Ruth's dog, didn't greet me. Marie met me in the front hallway. Dabbing her eyes with a tissue, she sobbed, "She's gone. About ten minutes ago. I'm sorry you didn't make it in time."

"Oh, Marie, don't worry about that," I replied. "I didn't need to see her draw her last breath. I'm just glad you were here."

We held onto each other for a few minutes.

As I approached the hospital bed, Bella-dog came in from outside. I picked her up and put her on the bed next to Ruthie. Instead of licking her hand as she had done all week, the dog turned her back on her owner and focused on me. Bella knew Ruth was gone.

Phone calls needed to be made to Ruth's son, David, the hospice, friends, and Ruthie's trustee, who asked if I would call a locksmith and the cremation company.

The Home Health Care agency caregiver checked in with work and was released for the day. Marie and I were joined by Ruth's other longtime friends— Loraine, Molly, and Colonel Betty, who opened Ruthie's address book and got

 Drug Disposal Tip:

If you've been working with a hospice team, the nurse can help dispose of the drugs according to the hospice's protocols, like the one developed by The Denver Hospice "Team Green." Federal guidelines recommend mixing liquid morphine or other medications with kitty litter or coffee grounds, putting the substance in a nondescript container, and throwing it in the trash. Using this approach makes the medications undesirable and unusable to drug abusers and keeps them out of the public water supply. Some drugs can be safely flushed down a toilet. Ask your pharmacist about safe drug disposal. For unused non-prescription drugs, keep in mind that agencies like Project C.U.R.E. accept donations of over-the-counter medications and medical supplies.
Christine Zanoni, Director of Performance Improvement, The Denver Hospice

busy. Everyone listed was called with the exceptions of names crossed out . . . names of people who had died before Ruth.

The hospice nurse arrived. She and Marie disposed of the drugs. They poured the morphine into a container of kitty litter and got rid of the rest in a concise, professional manner.

Periodically, one of us would touch Ruthie's forehead and exclaim, "She's still warm." And we were all then compelled to run over and feel her forehead. This went on for a couple of hours, until the body removal team from the cremation company showed up. Some of us read aloud from the Bible. Others merely observed the activity going on around them.

Ruth's son, David, called and told me that he was not making the trip to his mother's house, that he had been there the previous night and knew it was the end. I told him I didn't blame him. It was all a bunch of hens at the house, anyway.

A neighbor dropped off donuts. Marie and I dashed out to make copies of a picture of Ruthie, so we could all have one. While we were gone, Molly, Loraine, and Colonel Betty cleaned out the refrigerator. Molly remembered that Ruth stored booze under the sinks in the bathrooms, so that was all trotted out and placed on the kitchen counter. We marveled at the collection, which included a bottle of Boone's Farm Strawberry Hill (The 1970s *swill-du-jour*).

Hospice—What Jo Didn't Know

- Although hospice organizations have offices, **hospice is not a place.** It is a way of caring for people who are sick.
- **Hospice does not give 24-hour care in a patient's home.** Family and/or friends are needed to help a hospice patient stay in his or her home.
- **The hospice team is not made up entirely of hospice workers. The hospice team may include a friend** of a hospice patient. It is an honor to be on the team.

More About Hospice— From Those In The Know

- People often wait too long to enter hospice care. If a person gets into hospice soon enough, **it can lengthen the patient's life and almost always improves the quality of life.**
- **Hospice is not a one-way street.** If the patient or family does not like the care, or if their goals or condition change, they can "check out" of hospice care.
- **You can stay enrolled in hospice for as long as necessary**, subject to certain criteria.
- **The majority of hospice care is delivered *to* the person**, whether in their home, a nursing home, or an assisted living residence.
- **Most people want to die at home**, without pain, supported and surrounded by loving people and familiar things. **Hospice works to make that possible.**
- **A hospice team** consists of a social worker, a chaplain, a nurse, a CNA (certified nursing assistant), and a doctor (the person's own physician or a hospice medical director), who oversees the care but visits a patient's home infrequently. Those in hospice residences or other inpatient settings have more acute medical needs, so this is where the doctors spend most of their time. The hospice nurse is usually the coordinator of care.
- Depending on the hospice agency, **patients may be admitted to an inpatient setting** from home care for many reasons. This is typically prompted by some change in the patient's condition that results in their being unsafe at home, or the

care can no longer be adequately managed at home. An injury could be an indication of such a change but is not an automatic ticket to an inpatient setting.

- There is a **misconception** about hospice care **that it is passive care.** Hospice is proactive, holistic, and focused on comfort rather than cure.
- Hospice and palliative care are the only approaches to serious illness that **take into account the whole person AND the whole family.**
- Hospice staff can **help manage family dysfunctions and act as mediators.**
- Hospice provides **bereavement care** to a person's family for thirteen months after a death.
- **Hospice has a strong commitment to providing care, regardless of the patient's ability to pay.** Both Medicare and Medicaid have a hospice benefit in which all medications, equipment, supplies related to the terminal diagnosis, and the services of the team are completely paid for. Some insurance companies have hospice benefits, too. And most hospices are eligible to accept Medicaid and have fundraising programs to cover indigent care. Medicaid benefits vary from state to state.

"Those in the know" include Jennifer Ballentine of the Colorado Hospice Organization and Christine Zanoni of The Denver Hospice

More information is available online about hospice, specific hospice programs, bereavement support resources, caregiving support, and anything to do with end-of-life challenges at www.coloradohospice.org and www.thedenverhospice.org.

Independence Issues

Chick Fight!

RUTH AND I got into one scrape during our years of friendship, and it was when she was sick and on morphine. We had a fight about her attempting to drive or "operate heavy machinery," as mentioned on pill bottle labels.

We were loading up her car for an outing. I left the keys on the dashboard and went back inside the house. She grabbed the keys, struggled out of the car and hobbled with unexpected speed around the vehicle. She was sneaking into the driver's seat when I came back out.

"Oh, no, Ruthie, you can't drive,"

She had one leg in the car and was easing in behind the wheel.

"I just want to see if I can back the car out of the garage in case of an emergency."

Emergency? A CPR (cardiopulmonary resuscitation) directive was posted on both the fridge and the front door!

"Sorry, can't let you do that. You're on morphine." I gently guided her out of the car.

When I reached for the keys, she would not give them up. There was a tug of war, which turned into an attention getting struggle. Ruthie was grunting and I was chuckling.

At first I thought she was kidding but soon realized she meant business when she yelled, "This is *my* car, and I want to back it up. GIVE ... ME ... THE ... KEYS!"

I expected the neighbors to arrive any minute, prompted by the noise and the spectacle taking place on the driveway.

 Medical Note:

A CPR directive is posted inside a house in places easily seen by emergency responders who might be called for assistance. If the patient is unconscious, the CPR directive (completed by the patient, with a physician's signature) indicates refusal of cardiopulmonary resuscitation.

A CPR directive is one of several legal, documentary tools for "advance care planning." Other advance directives include the Living Will and the Medical Durable Power of Attorney. A great deal of confusion and heartbreak can be avoided if a person completes some subset of these advance directives.
Jennifer Ballentine,
Manager of Professional Programs,
Colorado Hospice Organization

(*A note from Jo:* In some cases, a posted directive is listed as a DNR, as in "Do Not Resuscitate.")

Suddenly the grappling stopped.

She collapsed on the trunk and sobbed, "I'm so frustrated. This is so hard. I only wanted to know I can still drive my car."

Resignation chipped at my resolve, but my resolve was strong.

I hugged Ruth and helped her get into the front passenger seat. After I got in the car, we sat in silence. I looked at her. She glared at me.

"Are we still buddies and pals?" I smiled.

"I guess," she replied, clearly still disgruntled.

 Police Blotter:

A person who takes the car keys away from a licensed driver could be found guilty of theft or harassment or, depending on the size of the wrestling match, assault. But if you make an effort to prevent someone who is unable to safely operate a motor vehicle from getting behind the wheel, the police might give you an award. *Captain Parris Bradley, Criminal Investigations Commander*

The What-Si-Doodle

IT GOT TO the point where Ruthie needed someone to be with her 24/7. She refused round-the-clock care. I woke up one morning on a mission. I pledged to myself that I would, that day, at least arrange for Ruth to be connected with a medical-alert service.

Whether she liked it or not.

Since she slept half the day, I had time to find a company in the phone book and make a call. The man said he would come over in a couple of hours. Ruthie was still sleeping when he arrived, and Bella was on a walk with a neighbor, so Ruthie wasn't alerted by any barking dog. A gizmo was installed on the phone downstairs, and I was instructed on how to use the medical-alert system. We climbed the stairs with trepidation. I didn't know how Ruthie would react to me doing something like this behind her back.

She had gotten up and was coming out of the bathroom as I called out to her.

"Ruthie? Are you decent?"

"Not usually," she chirped back.

She looked at the installation man. She looked at me. I started talking.

A Tip From Jo:

About medical alarms: Look up "medical alarms" in the telephone directory or online. A set-up fee is usually required with a monthly payment. Fees can apply for pick-up service. A monitor is hooked up to telephones on each level of the house. The patient wears a necklace or a bracelet with a push button in case of an emergency. An operator comes on the monitor line and asks if everything is all right. If not, or there is no response from the patient, the alarm company calls from a list of family and friends provided by the patient. The first person contacted goes to check on the patient.

"Ruthie, this is Tom, and he's here to install a medical-alert system on your phone, so if you're alone and you need someone, you can press a little button and an operator will talk to you and then call me or Marie or David—whoever you want—and that person will come over and check on you, and this way you can still be independent but have help if you want it." I took a breath.

She stared at me as she processed the information.

"Would you like a bracelet or a necklace?" I asked her.

"Most people like the necklace, Ma'am," Tom interjected.

An eternal pause, until . . .

Ruthie pointed at the necklace. Tom slipped it over her head. Ruthie pulled it up near her face for a closer look before striking a pose.

With one arm thrust high into the air, she proclaimed, "I have a what-si-doodle!" Phew.

False Alarms

THINGS WENT SO well with the what-si-doodle that I assumed she would be up for a caregiver. I got brave and told Ruthie we should call some places recommended by the hospice. She dismissed the idea. She didn't want people she didn't know in her home. She was afraid they would steal her stuff.

I called her trustee and snitched on her. He said he would drop by the next day.

We three sat around the breakfast table, and Mark said, "Now, Ruthie. Years ago when you hired me to be your trustee, we came up with a plan in the event you reached a point in your life when you would need to have someone come into your home and take care of you. That time has come. You have the money. You have provided for this. Even if it's just for a few hours a day, you need a hired caregiver."

Nope. Not according to Ruth. It wasn't time yet. Good grief, she was stubborn!

Ruthie took a little bit of direction from her trustee, but she was still fiercely independent. She held on tight to her right to make her own decisions, and we, her friends, respected that.

However, the end was near.

 Home Health Care Tip:

It can be expensive to have round-the-clock care in the home. Some agencies charge as much as $600 or more per day for 24-hour skilled care. Shop around for a reputable and reasonable agency. If you have long-term care insurance, some or all of the charges may be covered.
Karen Paschal, R.N.,
Home Health Care Agency Director

Let's Call And Look Into It

I PULLED OUT the phone book to look for numbers of the services to which Ruth had first agreed and then reneged. She refused to hire anyone and would only allow me to make some query calls about assisted living arrangements.

Over the phone, I got the lowdown. Assisted living was expensive, cost extra for a dog (and even more for dog-walking service), and smoking was not allowed in the living quarters.

"A friend could always visit and take the tenant to the smoking veranda," the assisted living representative told me over the phone. "And another plus. When you reach a certain point, you may be moved right across the street to our nursing home!"

A cheery thought to some, perhaps, but Ruthie was not having any of it.

Her son called and asked if I had checked out assisted living.

"She doesn't want to go there."

"Why not?"

"Well, she can't smoke, for starters, and—"

David cut me off.

"She doesn't need to be smoking, anyway."

"Oh, c'mon, David. At this point, she's not going to cha—"

"May I speak with my mother?"

"Yes, of course."

I gave her the phone, pronto.

They had a brief conversation during which Ruthie unarguably confirmed that she was not a candidate for assisted living. Her life. End of discussion.

Instead, she wanted to move to my neighborhood, which was fine with me. However, I knew she wouldn't do it. Ruth called her real estate agent, who had endured countless "false-alarm house searches" for her over the years, and he set up a showing. I loaded Ruth and her wheelchair into her car, and we met the agent at the townhome. She could still walk a little bit and, at one point, left us alone in another room.

Realtor Tip:

Having a long-standing relationship with a real-estate agent can build trust and ensure protection from a bad deal.
Jeri Van Dyke,
Agent/Broker Associate

The agent whispered to me, "She can't be serious about moving. Is she in any condition for that?"

"She won't move."

And she didn't. On the way home, Ruth said she didn't like the place, and she never looked into relocation again.

May I Help You With Your Independence?

- There are people who have no problem **taking advantage of an elderly person.**
- **Nothing prevents a realtor** from selling a house to a person who probably should not buy one. Hopefully, most wouldn't do that.
- Baby Boomer Gary D., a realtor, tells about his **elderly client who bought a new condo, intending to downsize, only she put off leaving the old house.** "The client's health failed, and the person never moved to the condo. Then, she ended up in assisted living after having paid for two homes, including the condo HOA dues and utility costs."
- **If you are concerned about the well-being of a senior who lives alone and has no family (and won't accept help or advice from friends),** call the local police. They can refer you to someone who can help the senior. Some police departments have a senior resource advisor, whose job is to check on elderly citizens and help them resolve problems, put their affairs in order, and make sure they are all right. CAUTION: A fiercely independent elder might be offended that you "called the cops" on him or her and not speak to you again. For safety's sake, it might be worth the risk.

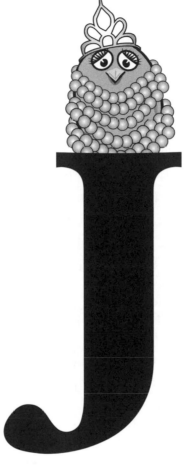

Jewelry Junkie

HIDING PLACES WERE everywhere in Ruthie's bedroom. Secret pullout panels in the bases of chests, cabinets with Chinese puzzle locks, and hat boxes that contained more than hats. Even so, she kept her finest baubles in the top drawer of her dresser, right out in the open. She had gorgeous rings, bracelets, necklaces, and brooches that she *said* she wanted to sell. However, the prices she wanted were higher than what the jewelers wanted to pay.

A jeweler friend of my husband made a house call one evening. We spread the good stuff out on Ruthie's bed, and she held court while he examined each piece. After a lecture on the evils of smoking, he offered her a price for the entire collection. She turned him down (as she lit another cigarette) because her jewelry was worth more, according to the thirty-year-old appraisals she waved in his face with her non-smoking hand.

 Jeweler Advice:

A person might get more money by donating jewelry to charity and taking the tax write-off rather than by selling it outright.
Paul Yacovetta, Jeweler

Later that week, my husband hand carried Ruth's glittery "bijoutry" downtown so a jeweler specializing in estate pieces could make a bid. The prices he quoted did not please Ruthie, either. So the jewelry went back in the drawer.

 About Appraisals:

These are written descriptions of jewelry specifying the replacement costs, usually for insurance claim purposes.
Paul Yacovetta, Jeweler

 Jeweler Advice:

Often, the highest return for used or estate jewelry is to sell the pieces to an individual who has shown interest in the items, an individual who is not a dealer. An appraisal might not be needed to sell jewelry—even to a dealer. But a fair market appraisal would be helpful as a good basis to use with an individual (something that could bring more than a dealer would offer).
Greg DeMark, Custom and Vintage Jeweler

Jettison The Jewelry

- The **prices listed in appraisals** are not what a jeweler would necessarily pay the owner to purchase the jewelry. "Appraisals cost anywhere from $60 to $150," says jeweler Paul Yacovetta.

- A jeweler might make a house call. However, most appraisals are done at an appraiser's office or store, because the jewelry needs to be cleaned, inspected, measured, and weighed with special instruments.

- "Although the most commonly written appraisal is the retail replacement or insurance appraisal," informs Greg DeMark, a custom jeweler specializing in vintage jewelry, "**of more value to the individual for resale purposes would be the fair market value appraisal**, which is based on cash value within a given trading area between a willing buyer and seller. Unless from a famous artist or manufacturer, **most modern jewelry from the mid 20th century to more recent vintage is not collectable** and, therefore, generally worth little more than the materials in the piece. For these items, it is best to get several offers from experienced and reputable dealers who would likely pay between 10% and 25% of the insurance value, depending on the item."

- "Another type of appraisal is used when a person wants to donate jewelry to charity, the **charitable donation appraisal.** It may or may not be less than the fair market value," adds Greg DeMark.

- **It is difficult for some people to hear that their jewelry isn't worth more. It's only worth what someone is willing to pay for it.**
- Typically, an elderly person's jewelry is outdated, so a **jeweler might buy it and take it apart**, melt it down or recycle the gold, and sell the stones in modern pieces.
- **Jewelers can sometimes give you the history** of a bauble, based on the date and place of purchase. Example: Before she died, my mother gave me a platinum ring she got for her high school graduation. A jeweler asked me where and in what year it had been bought. When I told him it had been purchased in the late 1930s in the southern U.S., he said it was likely made by a German in Argentina. "Platinum rings made in the Art Deco era were crafted by designers from Europe, and world events often prompted their relocation to a sympathetic South American country," explains jeweler Paul Yacovetta.

Keeping On Top Of The Meds

Not Your Grandmother's Pill Receptacle

ONCE A MONTH, Dad tracked Mother's medications. He huddled for an hour at the kitchen table over at least a dozen prescription bottles, carefully dropping pills into empty cylinders, each representing a day of her life, until they were full. Being a craftsman, Dad made this "wheel of pills" from his own design. It was a wooden lazy Susan-type dispenser that kept thirty days of medications neatly stacked and sorted.

It was an admired marvel. After Mom died, he donated it to the medical center so some other "lucky" patient could remain faithful to a pill-popping regimen.

Pain Management Tip:

Pain control is best achieved when medications are taken on a schedule rather than "as needed." It takes a certain amount of time for the pain relievers to be absorbed into the bloodstream and then be available to start working. During an acute pain episode, taking analgesics around the clock works best. As the pain cycle subsides, it is advisable to wean the patient from the medicines and then use them "only as needed."

Bridget Dunn, MD,
Teaching Physician

Driving Ms. Ruthie

RUTH WOULD NOT stay on top of her pain medication. She would wait until she was in an agonized state of palpitations before she took a dose. By then it was too late. She couldn't catch up.

Spasms were the worst. Ruth gripped the arms of her chair or a friend and grimaced with a sharp intake of breath, "I'm sucking wind here!"

These indiscriminate episodes of suffering knocked her inhibitions out the window, most times the car window.

Retail Therapy

WE SETTLED INTO a routine of dealing with the inevitable. Only it was never exactly routine. Sometimes I arrived to find my friend had painted on her eyebrows, ready to go somewhere. Anywhere. Her reason was, "I gotta keep a goin' if I'm gonna make a showin'!"

Thrift stores were frequent destinations. I wheeled her around. From her chair, she would wrestle something off of a rack for closer examination.

While holding a nightie up against me, she assessed aloud (a little too loud, actually), "This will just cover the valley of decision!"

"Ruthie! You're awful. Did you just make that up?"

She lifted a hand-painted eyebrow in response.

Making herself useful, she insisted that our purchases be stacked on her lap, saying "And you thought I was just another pretty face!"

On the way home Ruthie often requested that we drive by her former residences. She navigated us through the old neighborhoods as she critiqued current architecture. Sloppy workmanship on a remodel might evoke the remark, "Oh, for heaven's sake. That looks like a pimple on a secretary's chin." Judge Ruthie had spoken.

One time we were motoring along, and without warning, pain seized her face. Ruthie dug into her purse for morphine and squeezed some liquid on to her tongue. Within moments, her body eased and relaxed. She lit a couple of cigarettes, gave me one, and told me to smoke it. Ruthie prattled happily—or, rather, *yakked*. This was a "one-eighty" from her usual crotchety self on a tour of her city. Usually she complained about all the foreigners, bad drivers, and eyesores. As we puffed along, I told her she seemed stoned.

"I've never been stoned," Ruth said.

"Would you like to get high? We could pull over and try to buy some pot," I joked.

Only if it was a dying wish would I have seriously considered seeing it through.

"Har-dee-har-har," was her reaction.

I couldn't help thinking what it would be like, Ruthie high. She loved to smoke and laugh and eat Little Debbie cakes, so it made sense.

Come to find out, Ruth hadn't

 Police Blotter:

What if two ladies got busted sharing a joint? Depending on the location, possession of less than an ounce for personal use is a minor violation. The fine and insurance penalty for a conviction of driving under the influence of drugs? That's a lot different . . . and very ugly.
Captain Parris Bradley,
Criminal Investigations Commander

taken morphine. It was the drug Haldol that had somehow made its way into her purse. Haldol is for calming people who are in a fit of hysterics, freaking out.

Marie, a nurse and also a health care power of attorney for Ruth, was looking through her meds and saw it.

Marie was not amused as she asked, "Ruthie, did you take this?"

"Yes, it's morphine."

"No, it's not."

"Oh, well." Ruthie lit another cigarette. I felt a misplaced urge to cheer.

 Medical Update:

Haldol, or Haloperidol, is an anti-psychotic drug used to treat acute agitation, delirium, psychotic disorders, and Tourette's syndrome. ER Nickname: "Vitamin H". May be administered to unruly drunks. Haldol was part of a pharmaceutical care package from hospice.

Jean Marso, RN

Key Notes For Keeping Up With Medicine

- "**Reasoning can be distorted** by the actual disease or illness, pain, and/or the medications a patient is taking," advises Jean Marso, RN. "When distortion happens, medication errors and improper dosing can occur. One person should oversee the intake of medications for the person who is ill so as to avoid any mis-communications regarding when and what medication has been taken or given. That person, the overseer, should keep a log and write everything down with the dates and times the medicine is taken. A pillbox dispenser is a must for setting up meds."

- **Pillboxes and pill dispensers** are available at drugstores, medical equipment supply stores, and online. Prices can range from under a dollar to more than a thousand dollars on these items.

- **A top of the line dispenser** comes with bells, whistles, battery backup, reminder system, pill organizer, and locking mechanism to prevent pills from being ingested prematurely. When it is time for a dose, a buzzer sounds nonstop until the pills are removed and the drawer is replaced.

- How about an Italian walking stick with a Byzantine mosaic pillbox screw top? **Conduct a web search of "pillboxes"** for an amazing array of choices.

Dying While Doing Something You Love

Elder Fun And Games

DAD MET HIS girlfriend at the senior center. Ellie probably motivated Dad to live as long as he did. She kept him going. He danced with Ellie (as best as he could with those aching knees). He even drove at night. Those two were inseparable, like teenagers in love for the first time.

Not all of his daughters were comfortable with this at first.

"I don't want another woman around Mother's things," one of us worried aloud.

But we soon realized how happy Dad was—holding Ellie's hand, sharing bawdy jokes with her, hanging out together at the senior center. We became less concerned about Dad taking a wife and more concerned about his health.

 Estate Planning Tip:

Adult children might try maneuvering to protect their interests when their parent develops a new love interest. If the parent is competent and the deceased spouse did not set things up to prevent the surviving spouse from transferring assets, there isn't a lot children can do.

John N. McNamara, Jr.,
Denver Attorney

And Then It Happened . . .

DAD'S HEALTH WAS good for his age, 83. But he complained about dizzy spells. What if he fell down and hit his head when no one was around?

People were around when he fell down and hit his head. But nobody could do anything.

The old guys liked to shoot pool at the senior center. Dad got up from an observer chair (pub height, with a seat about thirty inches from the floor) to take his turn and went sprawling. He landed with such force that his hat, glasses, and ring flew across the room.

Ellie made it to the center in time to ride along in the ambulance. He told her his head hurt. They held hands.

Letting Go

THERE HAD ALREADY been some close calls, but this was it. Dad's tumble caused a massive brain injury with serious internal bleeding. He was put on life support.

The news reached me from across the country. The soonest I could join my family would be the following day. Through a series of phone calls, my siblings and I decided that the life-support machines should be unplugged. My sisters and brother said they would wait until I arrived, but I saw no reason to prolong the inevitable. It was time.

The plugs were pulled. Dad died inside of thirty minutes. His final vision on this earth was of some of his favorite people gathered around him, their faces filled with love and concern. Beautiful.

When Real Men Die

WE SPLASHED THROUGH puddles to reach our graveside seats. Dad's interment space was next to Mom's. (She had been buried during "southern monsoon season," too.) A few feet away there was a bench that identified the grave of their good friend, Ron Parks.

Mrs. Parks told us to sit there any time we wanted.

To his buddies of the older set, Mr. Parks was a legend because he died playing golf. He chipped the ball up on the green and said, "That didn't feel too good," and keeled over from a heart attack.

> **Bench Note:**
>
> Most cemeteries require that benches be made from granite, because granite holds up over time. There are teakwood and metal benches, but the upkeep and longevity is in question. Cemetery benches can easily cost up to $10,000 (inscription and installation included). Customization is also an option with imported stones, ceramic cameos, bronze release, and laser etching.
>
> *Larry Tabler, Funeral Director*

"L" For...
Let Each Moment Count

- Examples of **death during leisure** among my family and friends include dying while shooting pool, playing golf, taking a walk, riding the exercise bike, jogging, and mingling at a party.

- My childhood family doctor **suffered a heart attack during a reception** for a cardiology group. Right place. Right time. They brought him back. His wife died, ironically, while visiting a home where there had been a death in the family. She was holding dinner rolls in one hand, ringing the doorbell with the other hand, and was gone before she could move past the foyer. She died doing something she loved. Reaching out to others.

- **"I've had older folks die doing something recreational,"** says Joanne Richardson, Coroner of Summit County, Colorado. "A man in his 80s had a medical event and died while fishing. Because I needed to discern if his death was due to a medical event or drowning, an autopsy was indicated in this case. Most of the time, I don't order autopsies on people with significant health histories over the age of 60 unless the circumstances warrant it. I will order an autopsy on someone of any age if the circumstances surrounding the incident may have more than one explanation, such as the fisherman I mentioned. Unwitnessed deaths that occur during recreation may be precipitated by natural events, so an autopsy will help me rule 'natural versus accidental.' I've had people, age 50 and older, die while skiing, snowmobiling, and riding ATVs. Older people have also died in avalanches during participation in winter leisure activities."

- **If you happen to die while making love**, how nice for you—but maybe not so nice for the other person.

Meetings, Meetings, Meetings

Laying It On The Line

AT A TIME when Ruthie was still fighting for her independence, she scheduled a meeting of those orbiting closest around her. The hospice social worker, the nurse, and the nursing assistant attended along with Ruth's son, Marie (her neighbor and, as mentioned earlier, a nurse whom she had designated as a medical power of attorney), and me. Ruth called us to order.

"As you all know, I have been told I am terminal with cancer. I want to let all of you know that the word 'terminal' does not apply to me. Do not say it in my presence. I am going to fight this, and I am going to win."

The hospice nurse said that Ruth was making her own decisions and that we were all there for support. The hospice social worker nodded in agreement.

We covered many topics. Should Ruth hire someone to help her out a few hours a day? What if she fell down the stairs? How about finding a company that provides some kind of "alert" intercom system in case she needs help when she's alone? What about assisted living? What did she expect from us?

Ruthie was cagey about making any decisions, but she agreed to look into hiring some help and finding a company to provide the "alert" system. Marie and I tried to convince her that by engaging these services, she would be keeping her independence. David, Ruth's son, expressed concerns about his mother starting a fire with a cigarette. The nurse and social worker explained exactly what hospice could provide, which amounted to a nurse visit once a week, unless otherwise needed. Hospice would also send a CNA (certified nursing assistant) over twice a week to help with showers, sheet-changing, and laundry. Depending on availability, a hospice volunteer could come from time to time to help out with dog-walking, washing dishes, and other chores.

Even if we weren't on the same page, a meeting indicated what pages we were on. For the sake of communication, that was helpful in the days to come.

A Meeting After Mom Died?

AFTER MOM DIED, my husband pulled me aside and told me that I should suggest that my oldest sister, Carolyn, hold a meeting with Dad and the rest of us. This would enable the five of us to touch base and address any concerns before moving on with grief.

Apparently, families like my husband's have been known to do this sort of thing with great success when a parent dies, the oldest sibling leading the others. But not families like mine.

My family did not hold a meeting. We disbanded. Siblings, spouses, and children went home. That left Dad and me alone at his house.

> **Therapist's Tip:**
> Have a family meeting after a parent dies.
> *Vickie Kearney, MA, LPC*

Meet Halfway
Don't Halfway Meet

In therapy, you might learn that:

- After a parent dies, not only is it important to have a meeting, it is important to **have only biological (and adopted) children and family members present at the meeting without spouses or significant others (non-family members)**. It is always difficult to exclude people, but it is important to keep the numbers down to a minimum for decision-making purposes. Agree to take input from spouses and significant others but hold the meeting with only immediate family.

- A meeting after a death gives the family a chance to structure what needs to be done and offers a **chance for all to work together** to figure it out.

- The only chance family members may have to get together might be immediately after the death. **But if the meeting is scheduled after a few days or a couple of weeks later, it is probably better.** This allows some emotional distance from any grief reactions that may happen promptly after the death. Time helps people move their feelings from their hearts to their heads, where they are better able to think things through. This meeting should happen **no longer than one month** after a parent's death.

- **It should be clearly stated** in a meeting after a parent dies that:
  - ✓ There will be difficult times, and **open communication** is important if feelings get hurt or someone is unable to handle his or her part for a period of time.
  - ✓ All parties are important. **The biological and/or adopted children are going to be working together** with any input from spouses or significant others communicated through their partners.
- **Plan regular contact in time increments.** That might mean talking as a group weekly, monthly, or every four to six months for a time, depending on the needs of the family.
- **If a surviving parent doesn't set a meeting** (or there isn't a surviving parent), often the eldest child sets meetings. The eldest may be the formal leader of the siblings, but sometimes another child is the informal leader whom more people are likely to follow. The leader may be chosen by the sibling group.

Nemesisters
(And The Little Brother)

WITH DAD'S DEATH came a lazy regard for my sibling relationships. He was the glue that once kept us together.

Conversations with my sister, Julie, were awkward. My communication skills were grossly inadequate. I morphed into an inarticulate, frustrated wimp while she enunciated clearly and directly. Upon my arrival at Dad's house, Julie requested I not throw anything away, because her husband, Bob, wanted to sift through every trash bag. She told me that she and Bob were concerned that I might toss items of value.

Julie phoned in her requests. She did not come over and talk in person. But she did ask me to meet her and her husband for dinner—a dinner that ended in disaster.

> ## Positive Think Tip from Jo:
> Here's a little exercise. Replace the word "worry" with "wonder" and the word "anxious" with "eager." Then you're not so worried and anxious. Let's try that: "I *wondered* if my brother-in-law would come over with a bug bomb. And that's why I became *eager* and wedged chairs under door knobs." (Oh, yeah. Much better!)

At the restaurant, Bob announced that the next day he would set off a bug bomb in Dad's attic. This was supposedly on the agenda weeks before, so I told Bob it was too late for that, and I'd rather he didn't set off a bug bomb in the house since I was staying there and enjoyed breathing. Julie told me she didn't appreciate me yelling at her husband. Not much more was said after that. Our table got very, very quiet until somebody asked for the check.

That night I barely slept. Worry that Bob would go to the All-Night-Bug-Bomb-Store, buy a bug bomb, bring it over, and set it off at a wee hour kept me awake. Overtaken by paranoia, I became so anxious about imagined pest-control fumes that I wedged chairs under every door knob of the house. Rumination of fumigation controlled me.

Still, the work retreat at my childhood home was therapeutic. For me, cleaning provided cleansing of the soul.

Double-Takes

THE TIME CAME for all of us to come together and divide the furnishings. Carolyn and I watched out the window as Julie drove up, got out, and marched toward the house.

I remember hoping my sister wasn't armed. She didn't even say hello.

Julie glared at me. "You!"

(Me?)

"You are too intense. I'm not going to take your (bleep)." She plopped down in a chair.

I squeaked meekly, "I don't want you to feel that way . . ."

She demanded to know *what* I wanted.

"For us to get this taken care of in a more timely fashion. I'd like to see us being more proactive."

Julie flew out of her chair and mocked me. "Proactive? *Proactive?* That must be one of those fancy words they use where you live!"

With that, she stomped out of the room.

I looked at my other sister, my mouth gaping open, guppy-style.

Carolyn pleaded. "Jo, don't say anything, or we'll never get this done."

Julie came back, sat down again, and stated, "I know why Dad picked me for the executor of his will."

> **Therapist's Tip:**
>
> How to communicate with someone who is angry and you don't know why? 1. Say, "I feel like I've offended you. Is now a good time to talk?" 2. If the person says it's a good time, re-state, "I feel like I've offended you." 3. If the person says now is not a good time, ask when is a good time and set up a time to meet. If possible, have this conversation prior to making any decision with that person (like dividing up property).
> *Vickie Kearney, MA, LPC*

> **Therapist's Tip:**
>
> It is not healthy to "stuff" feelings. They need to be verbalized so the individual can understand what he or she is thinking or feeling. When, how, and with whom a person chooses to share is up to the person. Each person needs to feel safe. Eventually people need to talk in order to put their thoughts together and feel heard.
> *Vickie Kearney, MA, LPC*

A Tip From Jo:

In some large families, parents give each offspring an "estate duty." For example, the two oldest children or the eldest son and the eldest daughter could be designated as co-executors or co-personal representatives of an estate, while two other children might be named as co-powers of attorney.

Funny word "picked." I honestly thought she was named because she lived closest.

"He picked me because I'm the most level headed."

In an effort to keep the peace and a proactive pace, I shut my gaping mouth.

Wrapping Up The Loose, Frayed Ends

IMMEDIATELY FOLLOWING THE division of non-titled property, an undercurrent of irritation tugged on our family. Carolyn wanted to have a yard sale with the remaining contents of the house. Julie didn't. Anything of value that was not chosen, Julie and Bob loaded into their vehicles. I told myself I did not care because, after all, I had not selected those items during the division of the property.

We had a tough time agreeing on how to sell the house even without its contents.

The real estate agent came over and talked to us about an auction versus a sale. An auction would be quicker, he said. But Carolyn and Sammy felt the reserve price was too low. We loosely decided that an auction might be the best way to go. But not right away. And if the eventual auction didn't fetch the reserve price, no gavel would fall. We would stick a "For Sale" sign in the yard and take our chances. What's more, we were not unanimously satisfied with the real estate agent Dad had specified. We worked with him, anyway. However, when it came to the lawyer, the services of Dad's personal attorney were not used. Another lawyer was chosen.

The situation was tense.

My brother and his wife stayed another day so we could tackle the attic, but the attic tackled us. Daunted after a few hours by heat, brown recluse spiders, and the overwhelming amount of junk, we aborted the lofty mission. Confession: Before the project was abandoned, we committed a *coup de trash*. At the risk of upsetting the executrix and her husband, some garbage got hauled to the dump.

Dad once cleaned out the attic. He pulled his truck up near the side of the house and positioned it under the attic window. He tossed junk down into the truck bed: a broken Easy Bake Oven along with other dilapidated toys, moth-eaten clothes, melted 45s, some musty and dusty items, and a "football and gridiron" cradle he built when my brother was born. Then he drove to the landfill and added his discards to the stinky piles there. Nice and neat.

We should have done that, but we weren't sure it was okay to just dump junk off at the dump anymore. When we were kids, not only could you drop off, you could

 Police Blotter:

Is it legal to dig through a landfill/dump and take stuff? Sort of! It depends on the jurisdiction. Typically, when someone "abandons" property (with the exception of vehicles or real property), they forfeit their property rights to the item in question. The original owner of trashed property can't complain if someone takes an abandoned item, but if the owner of the landfill can profit from the discards, you can't take his property. You could be arrested for trespassing. Trash dumped alongside a road is fair game.
Captain Parris Bradley,
Criminal Investigations Commander

scrounge around out there. Dad and I unearthed bicycle parts from the dump so he could build me a bike, a bike that was better than store-bought.

I said goodbye to Carolyn, her husband Charles, and to Sammy and Robin. Then I settled in to finish out the week by cleaning and packing the items I had chosen to ship to myself. This included a large set of dishes that once belonged to an aunt. I chose them in the division process with my siblings and, afterwards, Julie, who was named after the aunt, asked me if she could have one of the platters. I copped an attitude (she could have chosen the dishes) and told her no, that I wanted to keep the set together. Carolyn tried to convince me to give Julie a platter, but I didn't budge . . . then. I sent her one the following Christmas. I never heard if she got it. She never let me know.

After the non-titled property division debacle, I headed for Carolyn's house to unwind before flying home and re-joining my own little family.

No Appointment Necessary

CAROLYN AND I treated ourselves to manicures and pedicures and walked into a "spa" (that's what the sign said!) for a massage. Not being "experienced massage-getters," my sister and I had no inkling that this "spa" was in reality a sleazy massage parlor until the *receptionist* left the reception area and didn't come back. We figured it out after looking around the room, noticed a cigarette burning like incense in an ashtray, and read the signs more closely. One instructed the therapists not to touch the customers' genitals. That was the tip-off. We guffawed and knee-slapped all the way home. And weeks later, when Carolyn told me that the place had been shut down by police in a prostitution raid, I felt lucky we weren't there at the time.

I began to realize that I needed more than a manicure, a pedicure, and a massage. I needed therapy.

 Therapist's Tip:

What does therapy cost? This depends on the length and depth of the therapy needed. Most counties have mental health centers that work on a sliding scale, according to people's incomes. Therapists in private practice vary in what they charge, usually $75 an hour to around $200 an hour.
Vickie Kearney, MA, LPC

Appointment Necessary

THE THERAPIST HEARD me blab and blubber. We role-played, with me portraying each of my siblings and her playing me.

When I asked if a heartfelt letter to Julie would be helpful, the therapist said, "Only if you never want to talk to her again. That's the risk you'll take if you confront her."

I took the risk in the form of an e-mail, asking Julie when we would know something more about Dad's estate and if she was going to provide family members with some sort of printout with numbers and an outline of what debts were owed to Dad and by whom.

Her reply that it was none of my business surprised me, because it seemed to me that it was everybody-in-the-family's business. Julie told me she would be happy to tell me what she owed Dad, but it was not her place to tell me what Carolyn and Sammy owed our father. Knowing she would eventually be required to come forth with the information for all of the heirs when the estate was settled, I let it go.

I made my sister aware that, in my opinion, her estate administration style left much to be desired. I wrote her a letter and sent it certified, so I would know she received it. I didn't want to wonder.

My letter said she was at risk of being perceived as untrustworthy and that it would be appreciated if she communicated more. Julie called to say she was offended that the letter was sent certified and that I labeled her untrustworthy.

Our relationship was crumbling.

Finally Some Closure

MY HUSBAND'S MOTHER had died a few years before my father, and following her death, my husband and his five siblings treated each other with respect. If there were feelings of resentment or frustration, those feelings were well hidden. John's sister, the eldest, carried out her executrix duties in an exact and forthcoming manner. All of the siblings were in the loop, informed to the smallest detail about what was happening with the estate. Any and all debts owed were revealed to all the surviving children. And when the personal (non-titled) property was divided, spouses were not in attendance. There was no offense meant and no offense taken.

Naturally, this is what I assumed would happen in my family when my father died. But it didn't.

A Tip From Jo:
Never assume.

How can this possibly be repaired? I asked myself.

Eventually, the estate was settled, and we all received inheritance checks minus any amount we owed our father. There was also an accounting from Julie's lawyer, based on figures provided by Julie.

Class Title: Family Communication Skills
Grade: N For "Needs Improvement"

Notes from a psychiatrist:

- **Sibling relationships** form and change over a lifetime.
- **Different factors flavor the relationship:** birth order, old (or new) rivalries, feeling picked on as a kid, or a sense of parental favoritism.
- Sibling relationships can be just as strained in adulthood as they were in childhood, and **the stress of a dying parent** will make it all worse.
- **We all think things through differently.** This can cause a lot of trouble in a stressed family, since you might assume that others in the family "process" just like you do. **Disagreements with family feel worse than disagreements with strangers.**
- Stress makes emotions raw. **Don't just watch what you say. Also watch what you hear.**

Dr. Gregory Kirk, MD, Psychiatrist

Obits
a.k.a. "The Women's Sports Page"

Small Town Dyin' Is A Bargain

IT COST FIFTY-FIVE cents a line to put my parents' obituaries in the hometown newspaper.

Because my mother died on a holiday, many friends were out of town and did not see the obituary and funeral announcement in the local paper until days after she was buried. Her obit was a basic biography listing where she was born, her survivors, an office job she had during World War II, and stating that she was a housewife.

> **An obituary** ("obit" for short) is the biography of a dead person. In the old days, a funeral announcement was the time and place of the funeral services. Feature obituaries are profiles of the deceased written in story form.
> *Gary Massaro, Columnist,*
> *Rocky Mountain News*

Dad's obituary was a little longer than Mom's because he lived and worked longer than she did.

There was no obituary for my friend Ruth. She didn't want one.

I guess you get what you pay for.

> **Jo's Obit Shopping Tip:**
> Funeral homes can set up obituaries and death notices, or individuals can do it themselves. I have discovered that the bigger the newspaper, the greater the cost. When I called a major New York newspaper, I was given a quote of more than $50 per line for a death notice, four-line-minimum requirement.

A Bit More About Obits

- Once free, obituaries and funeral notices are now usually **paid ads**. Most often, a family member writes them, and information is occasionally omitted (like the names of some surviving brothers or sisters).
- **To cut costs**, a family might run a basic death notice, stating the name of their relative who died and when the person died. Survivors might be listed without mentioning their places of residence.
- **When obituaries were free**, a newspaper clerk would type them, and an editor would "tighten them up" based on information sent from a mortuary instead of family. There was too much chance for fraud, like someone *planting* an obit in the paper about someone who is not dead yet.
- **Feature obituaries are assigned to reporters, or they find them on their own** based on suggestions from funeral homes or phone calls and e-mails from friends and family of the deceased. To have a loved one considered for a feature obit, call or e-mail the appropriate newspaper reporter with a paragraph detailing what was interesting about the deceased.
- "My obits are about common folks," says columnist, Gary Massaro, *Rocky Mountain News*. "One guy had such an unusual nickname that I had to find out why. To do that, I was obligated to tell his story. And believe me, **everyone has a story**."

- Feature obit writer, Virginia Culver, *The Denver Post*, says, "Even people whose lives seemed dull turn out to be interesting. While **some people want to have their loved ones remembered honestly**, warts and all, **others would rather bestow sainthood**." Virginia recommends that people ask their parents about their early lives or jobs, how they met their spouses, what it was like way back when, or if they survived some trauma or poverty. "Some are very good at knowing what their parents did, professionally or personally. Others don't have a clue."

- **Write your own obituary**. The following obituary ran in a Nashville, Tennessee newspaper. Printed here by permission from the decedent's son, it appears as it did in the paper (with identifying information omitted).

Gladys (last name)
Age 89
(date)
(county)
Of Nashville, (date of death). Survived by son David and his wife Judy, three grandchildren, and four great-grandchildren. "Hi Everyone, I'm at my Final Destination. It took me 89 years, 5 months and 6 days, but I finally made it. God walked me to the mansion and I didn't lose my breath one time. When we got there I got to see my husband Herschel, my daughter Pud, and my grand-daughter, Davina. Tears were running down my cheeks. I looked at God and asked the question, 'I thought there were no tears in Heaven?' He replied, 'No tears of sorrow, Gladys, those are tears of joy.' I'm not asking any more questions! I want to invite you all to my celebration of life. My son, David, will be doing my service.

I know it's rated PG, but at least I talked him out of charging admission. As far as pallbearers, I told David to get Ross and a two wheeler. But I think he's going to do it the old-fashioned way. Be sure and come, especially if it's a work day. This will be one celebration you don't want to miss. I love you and hope I see you all later. Take care of them Judy. Love, Granny." The celebration will be 11 a.m. Thursday. In lieu of flowers, donations may be made to the church. Visitation will be Tuesday 3-8 p.m. at the funeral home, and Thursday 10 a.m. until service time at the church. Arrangements by the funeral home.

If You Love Your Loved Ones, Pre-Plan!

Presenting Items To People Before You Go

Affairs Out Of Order

SOME DAYS I would walk in the door, and Ruthie would be full of "piss and vinegar" (her words). On other days she would greet me with, "I'm having a pity party." And she would be crying.

If anyone was entitled to have a pity party, it was Ruth. These episodes didn't last long, a half hour tops. And then we would be off on some organizational project as she continued getting her affairs in order. "Everything has a place and everything in its place" was her mantra.

Years before, Ruth had gotten her financial affairs in order with a trustee. She also had a lawyer and a Will. On those fronts, she was prepared. But she repeatedly said she didn't want to leave a mess at her house.

"Who cares?" I asked her.

"I just don't want to leave a mess."

"Okay, then. Let's get this place in shape!" That was the optimistic understatement of the year.

But we got busy. She would often walk into a room with some sort of intent written on her face, and then she would pause and say, "Now, I was going to do something wonderful . . ." Eventually, she thought of it, or not. That T-shirt with the saying *Why Did I Come In Here?* on the front would have been the perfect gift for Ruthie.

It was during one of these organization frenzies in her "Go To-Hell" room (Ruth's name for her office) that I saw Ruthie's big stash of money. I already knew about the little stash, hundred dollar bills in a bank envelope (who would EVER think to look for money in a *bank envelope?*), located conveniently in the top drawer of her desk. She had me pull from that pile to pay for groceries or get change. Plain old everyday mad money for Ruthie.

But she showed me another larger stack of bills she had "hidden" in a zippered bank-issued clutch bag that was nestled inside a pile of papers and legal pads on her desk—$3,000 at least. In cash!

I pirated her trustee's number from his business card on her kitchen table and called him on my way home.

"Mark? I'm a friend of your client, Ruth. She's got a stash of hundred dollar bills in her house, and I thought somebody else should know besides me."

"See if you can get her to put it in the bank."

"Right-o."

But, ohhhh, no. Ruth needed that cash for emergencies, she said. It made me uncomfortable because if she misplaced it, I was the prime suspect.

 A Trustworthy Tip from Jo:

Non-family members caring for a friend can avoid problems by sharing knowledge about hidden money or valuables with the person entrusted to handle the business affairs of the friend.

She misplaced it. I was the prime suspect. I arrived at her house one day whistling a happy tune with a skip in my step, ready to take on whatever she had planned, and she met me at the door with a scowl.

"I can't find the money."

"What money?"

Ruth watched me like a hawk as I looked for the money. It was right there where she had left it. She still refused to put it in the bank. Hey, it was her money. But I couldn't help thinking that a better plan would have been to deposit most of the money in a bank and create a method for managing things financially in an emergency.

Funeral Director's Note:

Open or closed casket? It's a matter of personal preference, and, in some cases, religion. It's the choice of the family, whether they want to share viewing before, during, or after services. An open casket may provide closure for family, friends, neighbors, and acquaintances. It's a connection for people to make, one last time.
Larry Tabler, Funeral Director

A Man Without A Plan

DAD PLANNED MOM'S service, which meant we asked what he wanted, made suggestions, and he had the final say. Open casket was the only option with my parents. It was the way their elders had done it, and it helped provide closure, seeing the person one last time.

Otherwise, Mom's preferences were not known. Dad struggled with some decisions. No one anticipated such a long day at the funeral home.

Meanwhile, back at the ranch, we found the cemetery plot deed in a drawer of the dining room hutch. My parents were not organized people.

That evening, the inquisition continued.

"Dad, would you like for us to stand up and say something about Mom?"

"No. No. I don't think I could take that if ya'll got up and talked about your mother. I'd cry too much."

Carolyn told Dad that when he cried, he sounded like a puppy. He stopped crying and chuckled, like a man.

Plan And Plot Your Own Demise

- **Pre-plan** means exactly that: plan, before you die, what you want to happen when you die.
- To **pre-arrange** means you arrange your pre-plan with a death care industry provider (meet with a funeral director; pick out your casket, or urn, or a shroud for a *green burial*; choose a crematory, ash scattering location, or other details).
- A pre-paid arrangement is when your pre-plan is arranged and paid for before you go.
- **The Pros and Cons of Pre-Paid Arrangement**
  - ✓ The pros? Locked-in prices. That *free* feeling that it's done. The pros are obvious, especially when you consider that most death care industry providers are professionals, trained to comfort and handle details for those in mourning.
  - ✓ Is there a con? Yes, if you don't know if a particular funeral home, mortuary, or crematorium will be in business when you die. "My husband and I pre-arranged and pre-paid for our funerals and burial decades ago," shares Kathryn, age 84. "Everything was taken care of when my husband

died. Since his death, the facility has gone out of business. Now, I don't know if my funeral expenses are still covered, even though they're paid for."

- **If a funeral is not pre-planned or pre-arranged**, it can take an entire day, start to finish, putting it all together at a funeral home. You could spend two hours with the funeral director, if the choices are simple, and two hours with the cemetery. Then you could end up going back the next day because there are so many choices. This is a great argument for pre-planning one's own funeral!

- Pre-paid arrangements with funeral homes can include **benefits for loved ones.** Example: With certain large companies, if a child or grandchild under 21 dies before you do, providing there's no lapse in payment, their funeral is free. Another benefit? **An endowment fund**, whereby the cemetery is maintained as a part of the package. If there is no endowment fund, cemetery upkeep—services like mowing or the repair of the statuary—falls on volunteers and family members.

- Pre-plan, yes. Pre-arrange, yes. **Pre-pay? Maybe**. Many think it is a good idea to make the plans for their funeral, burial, cremation—whatever—and set aside the money for loved ones to pay for it when it is needed. In some pre-pay situations, the money given to a funeral home goes into a *master trust*, but an increasingly more prevalent scenario has pre-paid arrangements funded through insurance companies, so the services can be guaranteed for the consumer.

- "In this death-denying society," philosophizes Baby Boomer Mike, "**parents who don't pre-arrange are setting their kids**

up if they expect them to agree on these end-of-life decisions. They need guidance. Even if you just tell your kids verbally what you want (that would be *pre-plan*), it's something—better than nothing!"

- **Remember, whatever you have pre-planned, tell your family and have them agree—in writing**. Even so, understand that *what you plan might not happen.* (Sorry. But, hey, maybe your loved ones will see it through. I don't know 'em, they're your people.)

Personal Pre-Planning Checklist

List contact names, addresses and all pertinent numbers for:

❑ **Funeral Home, Crematory** (if applicable)

❑ **Retirement Pay Information**   ❑ **Insurance Polices** (and value of each)

❑ **Bank Accounts**   ❑ **Safe-Deposit Boxes** (Who has a key?)

❑ **House Information:** Put papers regarding home ownership in a file drawer or lock box in the home *and* in a safe-deposit box.

❑ **Homeowner's Insurance**   ❑ **Automobile Insurance**   ❑ **Investments**

❑ **Medical Insurance**   ❑ **Lawyer**   ❑ **Tax Preparer and Filing Information**

❑ **Credit Card:** Put Personal Representative's name on this account with stipulations for use. Example: For use only to carry out the Personal Representative's duties—travel and expenditures—and once the duties are carried out, the card is destroyed.

❑ **Obituary** (if pre-written)   ❑ **Newspaper(s) for Obituary Posting**

❑ **Associations to be notified** for inclusion in obituary section of newsletters.

❑ **Miscellaneous Info:** Telephone service, newspaper delivery, family, nearest neighbor, friends, health club, realtor, estate sale company, veterinarian, church or other places where donations should be made.

❑ **Disbursement of Properties:** List specific items that go to specific people.

Put all this information, signed and dated, in a safe place.
Tell your loved ones the location.

Presenting Items To People Before You Go

Lady of the Ring

AS A RITE of passage, my grandfather bought each daughter a dinner ring of the Art Deco style when she graduated from high school in the 1930s. Like her sisters before her, Mom chose her own ring at the jewelry store. From the time I was a young girl, it was common family knowledge that I would receive Mother's ring by default, because my older sisters had already been given special rings by our aunt and grandmother.

About a month before she died, Mom presented the ring to me and said, "Don't let Beau (my oldest son) give it to no li'l ol' girl."

I promised I wouldn't, and I have worn the ring ever since.

 Therapist's Tip:

The act of "presenting" an item to a loved one before one dies speaks directly to the relationship, and each person may cherish the gift and the giver.
Vickie Kearney, MA, LPC

The Last Gifts

SOME OF RUTH'S friends took vacations at the end of her last summer. They dropped by before their trips to say goodbye. Ruth told them, "I doubt I'll be here when you get back." She presented them with gifts—a framed picture, clothes. She donated her father's military uniform to a collector. She knew it was almost time.

I felt honored, yet awkward, when Ruth proposed that her mother's engagement ring be given to me. She told me some of the details of her Will—who was getting what and who was getting nothing. I told her I did not want to be in her Will.

"Good, because you're not," she half snapped.

Fair enough.

It's All In The Presentation

- Later in life, some people begin to **give items away on special occasions** such as holidays, birthdays, or weddings. This can be a way of distributing items prior to one's death.

- Another way to distribute items would be to **discuss with people what items they would like** to have after you are gone. Use masking tape, markers or sticky notes (*really* sticky notes) to label these items individually with the names of the intended recipients. A backup list on paper to accompany this method would be a good idea.

- Dying parents or friends might **make a home movie** stating *what* goes *where* after they are gone.

Quilts And Other Ways To Celebrate Memories

Quilts

CURTAINS MADE BY Mother in the 1950s have now been transformed into a quilt by my sister, Carolyn. The funky lime-green and lemon-yellow fabric is forever ingrained in my memory, prompting intense flashbacks of sitting on the living room floor playing with my Susie Smart doll, watching out the window for a ride from a high school friend, or seeing a date come up the front walk and knowing he's going to have to sit down with my dad for a talk before we can go anywhere. It seems like yesterday.

From attic throwaways, my brother's wife squirreled away swatches of Mom's old leftover material from sewing projects and had a quilt made from squares of the polyester, Dotted Swiss, and kettle cloth. More like a time machine than a blanket, this quilt is a magical reminder of days gone by. Mother was an excellent seamstress. Not only did she make the clothes for the females of the family, she stitched the top for a pop-up tent trailer that my father designed and constructed. It was a project only suited for the big outdoors, and I was proud to see my mother sewing tarp-sized canvas on the driveway, until we took the first embarrassing family road trip vacation. When opened up, the cloth roof had to be secured to the sides, not with snap grippers as seen on manufactured campers, but with grommets and giant safety pins.

Other Ways To Celebrate Memories

DAD'S PRINTING ON letters and packages was a work of art. He drew guidelines for lettering and wrote in calligraphy—like a Leonardo da Vinci sketch. A few weeks before he died, I received a package from Dad and saved the address label, because it was a particularly fine sample of his penmanship. This was later scanned and used as the prototype for self-sticking return address labels ordered from a professional copy center.

My sister, Carolyn, ironed on photocopies of Dad's art—a painting and a drawing—to the sides of canvas bags and gave them away as gifts.

Not A Quilt—The Mother Of All Memories Of Dad

FOR POSTERITY, MY dad liked to make audio tapes of himself on his cassette recorder. After his death, I found an old, unlabeled tape and listened to it. On one side was thirty minutes of audio— a conversation between my father and his best friend, Carter, with running commentary during a long ago, college football game television broadcast. Dad must not have known the "record" button was on. To hear them argue about mail-in rebates versus in-store coupons and cuss uproariously over crowd noise and game plays brought tears to my eyes. I had copies made for my siblings and Carter.

Respect The Family Unit

DAD'S LAST DAY seemed like an eternity. His fatal injury happened a few hours after sunrise. By sundown, it was apparent that he would not pull through. The phone rang frequently throughout the day as I packed for the trip to my childhood home the next morning. Each time, I expected to hear my brother or one of my sisters on the line. But they were not making the calls.

Updates about my dying father came from Julie's husband, Bob. When I made comments or offered suggestions, he said things like, "We're not going to do that." My brother-in-law spoke as if he was the decision-maker for our family!

Surely, he was only trying to help, but I became irritated and asked why my sisters and brother were not calling me. After that, my brother became my contact person. My brother-in-law didn't call back.

 Therapist's Tip:

In-laws do best if they stay out of the decision-making process and should wait until they are asked directly by a family member. When a non-member makes a suggestion or a statement, it should be communicated through the family member with whom they have the closest connection.
Vickie Kearney, MA, LPC

 Therapist's Tip:

When a non-family member is "only trying to help" you might say, "I appreciate your help, however, at this point in the process I need contact with my siblings. So I will be in contact with each of them, and we can determine how best to proceed from here. Again, thanks for your help."
Vickie Kearney, MA, LPC

"If you ain't from the womb, get out of the room," my brother Sammy said under his breath when anyone besides immediate family tried to run things.

 Therapist's Tip:

Moving forward with a passive-aggressive comment like "If you ain't from the womb, get out of the room" would have turned the informal network of siblings that was *growing underground* into a more formal network. This would have been a good opportunity for all siblings to talk about the family members needing to act together and make decisions without any spouses' direct involvement.
Vickie Kearney, MA, LPC

Spouses, cousins, and friends probably meant well. However, Dad was *our* father, not theirs.

Which Way Went The Welcome Wagon?

DURING THE FIRST few days I was cleaning at Dad's house, my brother-in-law, Bob, called with a proposal. How about I join him at his work and help him out? Then, after I returned to Colorado, he would clean out Dad's house.

Seconds of silence ticked by until, with forced composure, I informed him that *I* would clean out my *own* Dad's house. "That's why I'm here, Bob. That's what I'm going to do."

 Therapist's Tip:

It's good to be direct and "stick to your guns" in this situation.
Vickie Kearney, MA, LPC

Long Division Problems

IN WHAT RESEMBLED a somber game show marathon with all contestants on edge, we took turns choosing furniture and household items. Julie's adult children were there. All of my siblings' spouses were there. I had no reinforcements and felt that was how it should be.

 Therapist's Tip:

Dividing property without stepping on toes? Meet together and take turns. Emotional value and financial value are very different. Discuss beforehand. Do it the White Elephant way. Put numbers on items. Draw for numbers and negotiate trades.
Vickie Kearney, MA, LPC

We took a break before choosing items from Dad's workshop. Bob had lobbied to keep the workshop together and move it, intact, to his place. He said he thought Dad would want it that way.

It didn't happen that way. The workshop items didn't interest me, but once I realized my brother would like to have them for his own *man house*, I asked Sammy for a list and then chose tools for my brother and me to "share and keep on his property."

Help Others Respect The Family Unit

- **An online auction** is another way to divide personal property. From the privacy of their individual homes, family members use points to bid (anonymously, in some cases) on items of sentimental value. Some estate lawyers can set this up.
- Try to **keep in mind what is beneficial to the family** as a whole.
- Try these three **steps to let a non-family member know you are uncomfortable that they seem to be trying to take charge:**
  - ✓ Thank the person for their help.
  - ✓ Explain that, as a family member, you would like to deal directly with your siblings.
  - ✓ Tell the person that you will get in touch with each family member and suggest the process of working together.
- Communication during stressful times might go better if you make **"I" statements.** "I think," "I feel," "I wish," "I want," "I need."

Respect Other Family Units

My "Brother By Osmosis"

FOR YEARS I observed Ruth's side of a love-hate relationship with her son, David. Nothing he did seemed to make her happy. If he gave her a gift, she only wanted a card. If he only sent her a card, she wanted a gift. And she could not forgive, let alone forget, much of anything. She didn't want to trust David.

Since Ruth would not trust her son—her only immediate family member except for her sister in California, with whom she had not spoken in years—I had worked hard over the past few months to gain her trust by being as open as possible about my own life. For instance, I plainly stated that I was not interested in her money and told her how much money I made, information I had never even shared with my parents. I told her so she would know I was not after her money. If Ruth tried to give me anything, I would offer to pay for it, and most times, she would let me.

I made the commitment to help her die in the manner she wanted, with dignity, in her home, "surrounded by her beautiful things"—the perpetual qualifying phrase Ruth used in reference to preparing for the end of her life. Because she said she considered me her "daughter by osmosis," I felt compelled to help in any way I could.

Helping Ruthie die was no easy task. Helping Ruthie *live* was no easy task, either.

Meeting My "Brother By Osmosis"

THE FIRST TIME I laid eyes on David, I was nervous.

> **Therapist's Tip:**
>
> When you're helping care for an elderly friend, keep his or her children in the loop, within the confines of the parent's wishes.
> *Vickie Kearney, MA, LPC*

David had been calling his mother, and I had been answering the phone. I didn't want him to think I was trying to take over or replace him as her adult child. To head off any such misconception, I insisted Ruth speak with her son each time he called. The phone would ring, and sometimes she would say, "Whoever it is, I'm sleeping." Ruth didn't have Caller ID and was often very tired or a little out of it on medication. But if her son called, she needed to take the call, and I told her so. After that, she took his calls without fail and seemed happy to hear from him.

Our first meeting went well. Ruth introduced me to David. We shook hands. He seemed to see that my intentions were good, that I was truly concerned for his mother's well-being.

The Sister's Letter

RUTH WAS ON her deathbed when a letter arrived from her sister, Margaret. We friends opened it and passed it around.

Taking turns, we read the letter to Ruthie. Margaret's words filled the air. Words about hearing of Ruth's "heroic battle with cancer" and hopes that Ruth was all right, wishes that Ruth would answer Margaret's letters and phone calls, and her desire that they could find their way back to being the fun-loving sisters from their childhood.

Each time the letter was read aloud, Ruth did not respond. She remained perfectly still with no expression on her face. There was no way of knowing for sure if she heard us, but we agreed that we believed she did.

Police Blotter:

Is it legal to open someone else's mail? Not usually. Intent is the issue. If your intent is to assist an elderly person with their personal affairs, who's going to complain? But if you're simply a nosey neighbor and you want to see what the people next door are up to, it's a federal offense. Start with permission. Make it easy on survivors. Designate somebody to act on your behalf if you can't act for yourself.
Captain Parris Bradley,
Criminal Investigations Commander

We called Ruthie's sister. After a couple of rings, Margaret picked up the phone. "Hello?"

"Hello, Margaret? This is a friend of your sister. She's in her last days. I wanted to let you know that your letter arrived, and we opened it and read it to Ruth."

"Do you think she would talk to me?"

"She can't, really. I'm sorry."

Margaret was quiet. After a moment, "Do you think I have time to get there? But I don't know if I can travel. I have this heart condition . . ."

"I'm afraid she might be gone by the time you get here," I told her.

"Oh. Would you mind talking to me for a little while?"

We talked. When I told her we were singing hymns, she told me to be sure to sing *Onward Christian Soldiers,* because that was Ruthie's solo at church when she was ten years old—almost seventy years earlier. Margaret said Ruthie had been "so cute" in a pretty dress, holding flowers, singing that song.

The phone got passed around. Margaret had met some of Ruth's other friends, and they spoke with her, too. Before hanging up, we assured Margaret that her sister was not in pain.

Later that day, when we sang *Onward Christian Soldiers,* Ruth's face softened, and her eyebrows lifted. Briefly. But it happened.

———

IN THE ENSUING weeks, after Ruthie's death, her sister and I talked often. Margaret was trying to come to terms with her loss and the fact that Ruthie died without their reconciliation. She asked me if I had seen a certain ring. She described it as, "A diamond in the center with sapphire baguettes around it. It was my mother's engagement ring."

I looked at my hand and confessed, "I'm wearing it." Ruth had left it to me. Silence.

There was only one thing to do. "And Margaret, I'm sending it to you."

The ring belonged in that family.

More R-E-S-P-E-C-T

- **Handle with care!** Estrangement might be an issue in other people's families, and you could find yourself stuck in the middle of an ugly set of circumstances.
- In increasing numbers, people are in situations whereby they are **helping to care for an elderly friend or neighbor.** This can be awkward for both the helper/neighbor and the family of the elder. **Open communication** is important.
- Here are some **ways to assure the adult child of an elderly friend** that you, a non-family member, are *not* trying to replace him.
  - ✓ **Run** decisions past him.
  - ✓ **Keep** copies of all signed papers in place for him.
  - ✓ **Ask** him what he needs and how he would like to be involved.
  - ✓ **Give** him pictures taken and letters written.
  - ✓ **Have** his phone numbers, address, and schedule so you can reach him.
  - ✓ **Provide** information about others who are helping his parent.
  - ✓ **Schedule** specific times to have contact with him.

  These suggestions are contingent upon an active relationship between the senior and the adult offspring.
- In dealing with an elderly friend or neighbor, **outside help from a *senior advocate* might be needed.** Call your local police department for such contact information.

Stuff, Stuff, And More Stuff

Surprises And Shootings

The Surprise Hits Keep On Comin'!

A Surprise Of My Own

A Super-*Duper* Surprise!

Ruthie's "Beautiful Things"

YARD SALE STUFF was stored in Ruthie's garage. Party clothes from the 1960s, primitive sports equipment like skinny wooden tennis racquets and bicycles with built-in baskets, chandeliers topped by wiry caps, and crocheted toaster cozies shared a deficit of space. Multiple duplicates of every known tool and gardening implement were organized among orange waterfalls of industrial-size extension cords, which cascaded from ceiling hooks. There was barely enough room for a car.

Ruth's house was crammed with lovely furnishings, tastefully arranged. Art displays gave the main level the look of a museum. Antique watercolors, plaster pieces, and an ancient Chinese coin collection adorned the entryway. A puff-sleeved peasant woman in a family room painting seemed to wink as she revealed one larger-than-life breast.

The kitchen was jammed with stacks of papers, and racks of pots, pans, and projects until there were no work surfaces available.

Everything had a price on it in Ruthie's basement. That included vases (or "VAH- zez," as Ruthie called them), figurines, bolts of fabric, racks of estate costume jewelry (from friends who had passed away), a chest holding nearly-new knickknacks that Ruthie used for last minute gifts, and a supply of wrapping paper that would outlive Ruthie. Visitors to this subterranean realm tripped over retired exercise apparatus, lamp cords, tote bags, purple satin covered bedroom chairs, suitcases still packed with age-dried cold cream and other petrified toiletries from long ago cruises, a cavalcade of coats and furs, lockers holding God-knows-what, and enough resort clothes to open a boutique. Everything but a velvet Elvis painting was down there. The basement was barely navigable, organized enough for maneuverability, but only if you walked single file. As Ruthie would say, "You could get *corns on your hips* walking around down here!"

Everything in Ruthie's basement was designated for consignment sales—too good for yard sales—but she didn't consign. (Evidently, she needed these items to display her collection of dust.)

If Ruth owned one of something, she owned fifty of the same item. On the upper floor of her house, Ruth had three coat racks bent over, weary with purses. Loaded shoe racks piggybacked on doors. Closets and dressers brimmed with more shoes, boots, bedroom slippers ("slippies" in Ruthie-speak), sweaters, and scarves. Belts coiled like snakes in heaps under beds. She owned sweat suits and dress suits and pant suits and denim suits, along with a never-ending supply of muumuus, housecoats, robes, pajamas, and sexy peignoirs (which, thankfully, I never saw on Ruth). Slacks and blouses overran guest room closets. A chest stocked with those little sleeveless turtleneck-type bibs most often worn under v-neck sweaters occupied the space at the top of the stairs—a chest full of *just dickies*!

Ruthie had every kind of hat. Feather, cowboy, vintage, leather, straw, lace, fur, and fur-trimmed. Baseball caps, visors, and turbans. And wigs. She had a large drawer full of antique gloves and mittens . . . and a muff. One dresser had a hidden drawer on the bottom that contained more gloves, the finer kind. This type of drawer was designed for hiding valuables, but Ruthie didn't always comply with design.

———————

RUTHIE DIED IN her home surrounded by her "beautiful things" just as she had always wanted. Her beautiful things got turned over to an estate sale company. Some of it went into an industrial sized Dumpster that was parked on her driveway. Most of it was donated or sold.

Stuff About Clothes

- **Aside from the usual** drop-off or pick-up donations, clothes can go to shelters.
- **Organizations helping women** get back into the workforce accept donations of business wear.
- **Hospitals** sometimes take clothing donations for use in certain situations, such as when patients check out and need something to wear on the way home.
- **Hats, scarves, and wigs** are much appreciated by charitable groups serving women undergoing chemotherapy. Check with a cancer treatment center in your area.
- **Vintage clothes and costumes** are sometimes needed at schools, colleges, and community theaters for plays and productions.

Surprises And Shootings

The Obvious Hiding Place

WHEN IT CAME time to clean out our aunt's house, my sisters, my cousin Mary Beth, and I rooted through the possessions. Aunt Addy and Uncle Burke had lived the good life. They had a lovely home in a beautiful neighborhood. They had traveled extensively and amassed gorgeous clothes, jewelry,

Police Blotter:

The most often used hiding place *and* the first place a burglar would look? A woman's underwear drawer. (Some thieves are perverts and like to look through underwear.)
Captain Parris Bradley,
Criminal Investigations Commander

and mementos from all over the world. And, like our mother (and Ruthie), our aunt kept everything. One large drawer held dozens of girdles, some with price tags still attached. Loose among the girdles, we found three rings and a necklace. Who would think to look for jewelry in a girdle drawer?

Police Blotter:

Don't get too clever when hiding items. You'll outfox your own memory. If you've got fifty hiding places, try to list them! If you have fifty pieces that need to be hidden, get a safe-deposit box.
Captain Parris Bradley,
Criminal Investigations Commander

In a somewhat ceremonious fashion, we divided the jewelry. Although she resisted starting the process, our cousin Mary Beth chose first ("oldest to youngest" made sense) and picked a small cocktail ring. My sister, Carolyn, was next and selected another small diamond ring. My other sister, Julie, picked the remaining ring, the dinner ring that was likely a high school graduation gift from Addy's father, our grandfather.

During "clean out weekend at Addys," we flipped through every page of every book on every bookshelf, because that's where Uncle Burke was notorious for hiding hundred-dollar bills.

Police Blotter:

Clever hiding places 1. Diaper pails.
A good plastic bag and a couple layers
of junior's business will generally deter
the cleverest thief. 2. A snarly dog's
doghouse. Hide valuables or cash there,
unless the dog himself might eat it!
Captain Parris Bradley,
Criminal Investigations Commander

What's This?

SORTING THROUGH A desk drawer, Julie came across what looked like an ink pen, but somehow it was different. Julie examined it closely, turning it over in her hand. Carolyn looked on, their heads bent down together. With a loud *pop*, it discharged, spewing a dirty, smoky cloud. The pen was part "gun."

Carolyn screamed, "I can't hear, I can't hear!" She continued screaming as she ran down the hall. I intercepted her

Burke was notorious for a lot of things, including his money belt crammed with hidden cash, his offshore bank accounts, and his money bags buried in odd and interesting places.

No hundred-dollar bills floated from pages we flipped in the books at Addy and Burke's house during the work-weekend. But my sister discovered something mysterious.

 Police Blotter:

Hospital personnel are required to
report various types of injuries,
including weapons' injuries. Anything
that ejects a projectile is a firearm.
BB guns, slingshots, howitzers, and
even little Mace guns disguised as
pens are all weapons.
Captain Parris Bradley,
Criminal Investigations Commander

in a doorway. She put her hand up on the side of her head, which drew my attention to her ear. It was bleeding. She saw blood on her hand and became hysterical. We were all hysterical by this time, gathered around Carolyn in a mini-mob. With forced calmness, she announced loudly that she could hear again and headed for the bathroom. She relaxed as she looked at her reflection in the mirror. Only her earlobe had been nicked by a gob of decades old, congealed Mace that had solidified into a rock-hard bullet.

The wound did not appear to be serious. Still, we discussed a trip to the hospital. Mary Beth put the kabbosh on that, pointing out that when someone gets shot, there has to be an investigation. We didn't want the police to get involved! Plus, there was too much work to do, and Carolyn was willing to keep working, despite her injury.

Surprise Police Blotter Addendum:

"If the mishandling of a weapon or an accident results in the injury of another person, the shooter could be in trouble for something between assault and reckless endangerment, depending upon the level of the injury," according to *Captain Parris Bradley, Criminal Investigations Commander.* "If the projectile from the Mace gun/pen had hit the eye instead of the ear, the shooter could have been arrested, and the DA and/or a jury then would have decided if the shooter should be held criminally liable. So, yes, if there had been a trip made to the hospital, the police would have been called, and somebody could have been charged with a crime. It's not a crime in this situation to not report what happened, providing the victim made a conscious decision not to do so. But if someone of minor age or someone who is incapable of making a report is injured, then everyone who fails to call or assists in the cover up is liable for conspiracy to cover up a crime after the fact."

The Surprise Hits Keep On Comin'!

An Unexpected Gift

AFTER THE DUST surrounding Ruth's passing settled, her trustee called to arrange for the purchase of her car by my son, "Darling Beau," as she called him. We agreed on a price and set up a time for the transaction.

"And one more thing. Since your name is on Ruthie's checking account, that is your money, whatever's there and possibly the contents of the safe-deposit box. Do you have a key?"

"No, I turned that over to you with the checkbook and everything else."

Mark asked if I would meet him at the bank.

Ruthie's banker checked our IDs and escorted us into a vault. When Mark asked if there was anything in the joint box, I shook my head no. I looked at the banker and could have sworn she gave me the fisheye. She said nothing as the box was unlocked, revealing . . . nothing.

> **$ Bank Notes:**
>
> A signature card on a bank account overrides a Will. If the account is set up "joint with right of survivorship," the account is considered owned by both parties. Either party may transact business on the account. If one of the parties dies, it is automatically owned by the surviving party. If the account is set up POD (payable on death), the funds are given to the named person upon the death of the owner. On a POD, the receiver does not sign the signature card. They are the beneficiary in the event of death and until that point have no ownership of the funds. They cannot write any checks on the account until the owner dies. If a box is rented in both parties' names, it is considered a "joint" box. If one party dies, the survivor has rights to the contents.
> *Laura A. Tellor, Bank Vice President*

> **$ Bank Notes:**
>
> Use CAUTION with a joint safe-deposit box. For example, suppose Grandma explains in her Will that she intends to leave her jewels to the grandchildren. Somehow the jewels get into the box at the bank. If a friend is a co-owner of the box, when Grandma dies, the friend gets the jewels.
> *Laura A. Tellor, Bank Vice President*

A Surprise Of My Own

I HONORED RUTHIE'S memory by doing something nice for my sister, Carolyn, who was there for me when I needed to talk about my sick friend. We spent many hours on the phone talking about Ruthie. Carolyn gave me advice while Ruth was living and solace when she died. So I used some of the little Ruthie windfall to buy my sister a used piano. A piano was an instrumental part of growing up in our home, and Carolyn was the only daughter who didn't have one.

My sister's best friend, Judy, was a willing accomplice. She found a piano in Carolyn's town, and I bought it over the phone. Using a concocted excuse, Judy got Carolyn into the showroom, and they noticed a giant bow on a pretty little French Provincial style piano at the end of a row of consoles.

"Looks like someone is getting a piano for Christmas," my sister said.

"That's your piano, Carolyn. You're getting a piano for Christmas. It's from Jo."

Correction. It was from Ruth.

A Super-*Duper* Surprise!

The Siblings Give it One More Try

A YEAR AFTER Aunt Addy died, I was spending a week at Carolyn's house. She thought it would be a good idea to get all the siblings together. It would be the first time in many months, and we weren't sure Julie and Sammy would even show up. But they did, for a little family reunion weekend.

It was awkward at first. We had not been together in a while. Even though much oil and water had rushed under the bridges since Mom and Dad and Addy had died, we actually spent quality time together, as far as I could tell.

It felt like we were a family again. Julie played the piano while Carolyn and I sang. Sammy made a splash as guest host of the hot tub. Julie discussed her upcoming retirement with me. She expressed concerns about finances.

"Don't you think you'll inherit some money from Aunt Addy?"

"Well, I know my name is on a savings account," Julie said. "I thought I might just roll that back into the estate."

"Why would you do that? If you inherit it, it's yours." Then I zeroed in. "I heard that the three of us sisters and Cousin Mary Beth were named in Addy's Will."

"I heard that, too," Julie said.

"Don't you think that would upset Mom, that Sammy wasn't named?"

"Oh, Mom would be furious."

MOM WOULD HAVE been furious not only because she was a stickler about fair treatment for her children, but also because all of us had been close to Aunt Addy and Uncle Burke.

When we were young, we often spent a week or two with Aunt Addy and Uncle Burke during summer break. These were great times for us. Aunt Addy treated us as only an aunt—who doesn't have to live with you day in and day out—can. Uncle Burke was loud and fun. He handed out nicknames. Mine was *Junebug*, which I loved. He talked like the cartoon rooster, Foghorn Leghorn, and had a unique way of viewing the world.

Once, when Uncle Burke was teaching me to shoot a rifle, I fell down on my backside from the rifle's kickback. Uncle Burke could see that I was not really hurt, and instead of rushing over to tend to me, he doubled over, laughing. On another visit, I accidentally walked right into the patio door. As I rubbed my face, which stung from the direct frontal assault, Uncle Burke teased, "Does your face hurt? It's killing me!"

Aunt Addy survived Uncle Burke by almost 20 years. We remained close to her after his death. It seemed implausible that Sammy would be excluded from the inheritance, but then, none of us had seen the Will yet.

The weekend ended on a good note. Sam and Julie drove off as Carolyn and I waved goodbye, feeling hopeful that, despite the deaths of the elders, our family unit would survive.

What The . . .?

WITH THE NEXT day's mail delivery came a different feeling that can't be named—shouldn't be named. Carolyn held a letter in her hand.

"You better sit down," she said.

I sat down and listened as she read aloud Aunt Addy's Will. It became surreal as it became apparent. Our sister, Julie, was the sole heir. The Will was dated 1964.

I did the math. Our aunt and uncle had bequeathed their entire estate to Julie when she was 11 years old.

What I Learned From My "S"s

- **Surprises** happen. **Surprises** can be good, bad, or good and bad.
- **It's not *what* happens to you, it's what you *do* about it.** Sometimes there is nothing you can do or say.
- **Unwelcome surprises** after a parent's death might include:
  - ✓ **Debt** you didn't know about.
  - ✓ **Scams.** Example: Based on information from newspaper obituaries. A scammer might **call a deceased person's survivor (in many cases, the widow), and claim to represent a company that is owed money by the deceased.** Call the local Better Business Bureau to expose these phonies. Another example: **Identity theft** using the decedent's personal information.
  - ✓ Finding out that she or he was previously married, and you have **a half-sibling you didn't know about.**
  - ✓ **A woman you have never seen before attends your father's funeral** wearing a skimpy red dress and heavy makeup.
- I, myself, am leaving some **surprises**. Notes, poems, and letters in envelopes to be opened after I'm gone.

Time Waits For No One

If You Got 'Em, Smoke 'Em

MY MOM WAS a smoker. Toward the end of her life, it was about all she enjoyed.

When I visited my parents during my mother's illness, I would load her up in the car, toss the wheelchair in the trunk, and take her out for "smoky treats." This always upset my sisters, who would say, "I know you're taking Mother out so she can smoke!" As if Mom and I were carousing or getting pierced navels and tattoos.

Dad wouldn't let her smoke but surely knew she was sneaking cigarettes. All the breath mints and hand lotion in the world couldn't cover up that distinctive smell.

Dad knew about the lure of cigarettes. He smoked for years before he quit. While a heavy smoker, he stacked old newspapers by his side of the bed at night. He coughed enthusiastically first thing in the morning, spit it on the stack, and rolled it up in the top layer of paper for easy cleanup.

Any time I reminded him of his *hacking heydays*, he said, "My generation smoked before we knew it was bad for you." (His generation thought smoking 'til you brought up phlegm was *good* for you?)

Since smoking was taboo, my mother rolled herself into the bathroom for smoke breaks in the home. Of course, we all worried she might burn the house down with her and Dad in it, but that's not how she died.

 Police Blotter:

Your spouse dies in the bathroom, but you don't want them to be found there. You move them to a bed and then call the police. It's not "illegal," but you're in for a long day. If the police respond to a DOA (Dead On Arrival) call and the marks on the body don't match the position of the body, there's going to be a significant investigation as to why. Police are paid to be suspicious.
Captain Parris Bradley,
Criminal Investigations Commander

Death Takes No Holiday

MOTHER DIED ON Memorial Day. First thing in the morning, she wheeled into the bathroom and didn't come out. Dad woke up and checked on her. When she didn't answer through the locked door, he broke in. He found her in the wheelchair with her head balanced on the side of the sink. Heart failure.

The cry of the ambulance woke our neighbor and Dad's best friend, Carter.

He jumped out of bed, followed the sirens up the street, and accompanied Dad to the hospital. Carter was the talk of the town that weekend. He forgot he was still wearing his pajamas.

My sister's voice on the phone awakened me. "Mom's gone."

 Police Blotter:

A death in the home? Call 911. In most locations, that will get you a rescue unit and the police. The rescue people will hook up their equipment and figure out the person's actual condition. The job of the police is making sure the person did not die with assistance. An exception would be a hospice situation. The hospice people make it very clear what you should do and who you should call when an anticipated death occurs.

Captain Parris Bradley,
Criminal Investigations Commander

When Someone's Time Is Up . . .

- **It's natural** for survivors to think about things they wish they had (or had not) said. Savor the time spent together.
- **Think about that person's wishes,** how they would want to be treated, and how they would want situations to be handled.
- Help a dying person **enjoy the time remaining.**
- If you know the end is near for someone you love, **tell them how much you love them and reminisce about the special moments you had.** Here is one strategy for closure provided by Baby Boomer Jason. "If you know your parent is going, use the time remaining to talk about the cool stuff, the good memories, the great things he or she did. Talk about what you enjoyed, admired, what that person gave you. Look for those things. Make that the conversation rather than a long goodbye. That's what I wish I had done the night before my father died."
- Captain Parris Bradley, Criminal Investigations Commander, shares **other things to consider when someone's time is up:**
  - ✓ "The Police cannot, more like, *should not*, move a body. They have to wait for someone from the coroner's office to arrive (this could vary by state).
  - ✓ Occasionally someone in a hospice situation will call 911. Once the ball is set into motion, however, the rescue units and the police are obligated to respond and play by their own rules, not the rules of hospice.
  - ✓ If the caregiver is not a family member, the police might want to know if the medication was correct. Was the dose accurate? Did the pharmacy make an error? It can go on and on."

Death Is Quite An Undertaking

MY GRANDFATHER WAS an *undertaker* (the old-timey word for *funeral director* and *mortician*). Pappa Jep's family-operated funeral home was located in a two-story house. Living quarters were upstairs. The funeral parlor, embalming room, casket display area, an office, and a room in the back with a radio where workers and friends congregated were on the main level. The company vehicles included one hearse, a van to transport flowers to the cemetery, and ambulances. Sixty-plus years ago, ambulance service was often under the umbrella of a funeral home.

The Undertaker's Ambulance:

It was a funeral coach, maybe a Cadillac, with a red light on it. OSHA changed all that, thank goodness, in the 1960s. When all the safety features entered the picture, the funeral homes couldn't afford to meet the standards and happily turned ambulance service over to the fire department.
Larry Tabler, Funeral Director

Because ambulance service was not expensive (as cheap as five dollars a call), it was a common sight to see a new mother and her baby come home from the hospital in an ambulance provided by a funeral home.

"Mother, Stop Talking."

MY MOTHER TOLD stories about her brothers scaring the living daylights out of the funeral home cleaning crew. The best was the story of one brother who stretched out under a sheet on a mortuary slab, still as a stiff lying in state. He waited for the janitors and then moaned as he slowly . . . rose . . . to . . . a . . . sitting . . . position.

Mother boasted that our grandfather was an undertaker with a conscience. "During the Depression, Daddy didn't cut corners like other undertakers who stuffed bodies with newspapers, which made the skin turn gray."

A cousin, now in his seventies, worked for our grandfather when he was a young teenager and remembers a man who also worked there. "This guy was a well-known hand shaker," my cousin told me. "In those days, the hospital gave limbs that had been surgically removed to the funeral home (for burial). The hand shaker got hold of a hand amputated above the wrist and put it up his sleeve. As a gag, when someone shook his 'hand,' he let it go." (That would be a *gag*, all right!)

Another recollection from my first cousin: "It was the custom back then that bodies were taken to the home for a wake before the burial. When Mama Jep died, her body was brought to the house. People visited and paid their respects. That night, some of the family said they were going to 'sit up' with the body all night. Papa Jep informed them that unless they were also going to 'sit up' the next night at the cemetery, they weren't going to 'sit up' with the body that night."

Apparently, my grandfather made sure his people were sensible about death, and he didn't tolerate shenanigans—at least, the shenanigans he knew about. If he had known about the horseplay that actually took place at the funeral home, he would have been mortified.

> **? Questions for a Funeral Director:**
>
> Stuffing a body with newspapers? Is that an urban legend? "Here's how it might have happened," explains *Mike Hawkins, Funeral Director.* "In an autopsy procedure, the entire set of internal organs—the viscera—is removed for dissection. When the organs are removed, a substance—normally, absorbent cotton—is used to stuff the body. Unscrupulous undertakers have used newspapers (among other things) to fill the body cavity. But that wouldn't turn the skin a gray color. That's more of an urban legend—newspapers on the inside affecting skin color on the outside."

What "U" Taught Me

- Apparently, in this day and age, **you do not call a funeral director or a mortician an "undertaker."** (I wish I'd known that before interviewing a few while writing this book. Ex-cu-u-use *me!*)

- **"You can't make a dead man smile."** That's not a country and western song title (though it might make a good one, come to think of it). More than one mortician has told me that it is almost impossible to manipulate a facial expression after death. Key words, *almost impossible.* A skilled mortician can create a nice closure of the mouth and—with tissue fillers, restoration experience, and time on his or her hands—turn a frown upside down.

- **The death care industry has come a long way.** Caskets, urns, and other **products may be ordered online.** Baby Boomer Pamela knows from experience. "When my mother passed away, my sisters and I surfed the Internet and got some quotes. The next day we went to the funeral home and looked at caskets there. We ended up buying from a casket store on the Web and saved over 50% of what we would have paid at the funeral home. We ordered one day, and the casket was delivered directly to the funeral home the next day. I wouldn't hesitate to do it again."

- The industry has not only come a long way, it has gone full circle, one could say, with green burial. **What is green burial?**

About Green Burial

"IT MAY SOUND new, but this **environmentally-friendly** process has been around for . . . forever," says John Wilkerson, steward of The Glendale Memorial Nature Preserve in Florida. "We offer burial and cremation repository sites on preserved land. Our definition of green burial is no embalming fluid, only biodegradable caskets, and caskets aren't even necessary. A blanket or shroud works just as well. There's no vault used in the burial process. Markers are allowed if they're flat on the ground and measure up to four square feet—only two markers per thirteen graves. And pets can be buried in the family space."

When I spoke with Joe Sehee of The Green Burial Council, I really got an historical earful. **"For thousands of years, and up until the American Civil War in this country,"** Joe informed me, "when the 'better dying through chemistry' era was officially ushered in via the practice of embalming, most of humanity cared for its dead in a somewhat environmentally sensitive way. Just as midwives, several decades ago, began questioning the medical profession about the way babies were being born, a new breed of 'death doulas' are now leading the way in helping Americans challenge the death care profession."

Joe Sehee shared more about his organization.

"The Green Burial Council is **a national network of conventional cemetery and funeral providers** willing to accommodate families interested in more simple, sustainable, and participatory end-of-life rituals due to growing interest in burial that does not require the toxic practice of embalming or waste resources like concrete, metal, and hardwood through the use of burial vaults and coffins. People may even choose to allow their last act on earth to help facilitate the acquisition, restoration, and stewardship of natural areas by patronizing the Green Burial Council's certified 'conservation burial' grounds."

It Takes A Veterinarian And A Village

I ABOUT FAINTED when Ruth said that when she died, her ashes were to be scattered with those of her dog, Bella—who was very much alive.

"You can't be serious," I said.

"I would like my little girl (dog) with me when I tiptoe away. She's my dog, and no one else will take care of her like I do."

I asked, "What veterinarian would kill a perfectly healthy dog so the dog can join the master in the afterlife?" and added, "I'll do my best to prevent it."

Animal Doctor Q&A:

Would a veterinarian honor the request of a dying person to put down a pet so the ashes could be scattered with the owner's cremated remains? *Dr. Kevin Fitzgerald of TV's "Emergency Vets"* says a majority of veterinarians, including him, would say no. "This is a noble idea, to embark together. It was done with the pharaohs and Viking warriors. It's wrongheaded and selfish. We at Alameda East Veterinary Hospital in Denver don't put healthy animals to sleep. If they're destined to be together with their owners, why wouldn't they just catch up with them later?"

Someone else who would never allow Bella-dog to die before her time was Jim. Jim and his wife, Vonda, were the designated dog-walkers of "Team Ruth," friends and neighbors who were on call, day and night, to lend a hand. In the end, Ruthie bequeathed Bella to Jim and Vonda, along with an inheritance to take care of the dog through the end of her natural life.

A second opinion:

"How can any pet owner make such a disrespectful decision that a pet in good health be euthanized after the owner's death?" asks *Dr. Brenda McClelland, Veterinarian and Animal Communicator.* "They are essentially reducing their 'baby'—their lifetime companion—to nothing more than a mindless bundle of fur and bones. Can anyone prove that pets do or do not have a concept of death? No. I encourage all owners to have multiple plans lined up to help their pets after they die. Friends, family and rescue groups are all possible adopters. Ask your veterinarian to recommend a potential adopter. This can put your mind at ease that the new home will care for your pet as well as you did."

The Village Volunteers

RUTH'S NEXT-DOOR neighbors took care of her lawn and sometimes allowed her garbage to be added to theirs on pickup day. But most of that summer Marie or I loaded big smelly trash bags into our cars and drove them to the trash cans in our garages. Ruth refused to pay for removal, because she felt it was ridiculous paying for what, in her mind, should be free.

"Ruthie, it costs what? Six dollars a month?"

"Who cares? It's the principle."

Other neighbors helped out, too. But Ruth's closest friends got her through to the end on the most personal level. Marie, a nurse, was a friend of ten years who lived up the street. Colonel Betty was a friend of many more years, and she was also a nurse, of the retired military variety. Colonel Betty had run a M*A*S*H unit in Vietnam. (Ruth named these ladies her medical co-powers of attorney.)

Another friend of Ruthie's was Lorraine, a whirling dervish of energy, always dashing over with gifts and gallons of carrot juice. Lorraine was convinced that carrot juice killed cancer, and Ruth drank it down.

Police Blotter:

It is illegal to add your trash to someone else's garbage if you are not paying for the removal of the garbage. It's called *theft of services,* and prosecution is usually determined by the frequency of the violation and the amount of trash. It's a fine line between cleaning up litter (tossing a candy wrapper in a Dumpster) and stealing a service (dumping massive refuse in a Dumpster or a neighbor's garbage can). Theft of services can be proven when the prosecution shows scheme and design that one deliberately avoided paying for the service.
Captain Parris Bradley,
Criminal Investigations Commander

They were like sisters with a long history and short fuses between them. They yelled at each other a lot. Or, more accurately, Ruthie yelled at Lorraine. Lorraine was hard of hearing. Mostly, Ruthie yelled at Lorraine to go get some hearing aids!

It was Lorraine who convinced Ruth to put my name on her checking account. I had been writing out the checks for Ruth's autograph, but we all knew there would come a day when she would not be able to do something as simple as sign her name.

Other Ways **V**illagers Can Help

Under the direction of the elderly neighbor living alone:

- Neighbors can **work together**. Discuss concerns and alternative solutions.
- Offer to **make and deliver meals** following guidelines of a pre-arranged schedule.
- Offer to **run errands** and **provide rides** to doctor appointments.
- Grow a **phone tree** for needs and emergencies. List contact names and numbers.
- **Check on your elderly neighbors** regularly.

The Will: Write It Down, Make Your Wishes Known

Do Something, Even If It's Wrong

MONTHS CRAWLED BY after Dad's death, during which nothing was done with his house. I took a leave of absence from work and returned to my childhood home to clean and organize Dad's things. The culmination of this work would be the division of Dad's non-titled property between my siblings and me.

 Therapist's Tip:

Convince an elder to write down their wishes. Make this a special, easygoing time. Go out for coffee, sit down with tea, go away for a weekend, or go out to dinner. Ideas: 1. Create an easy-to-fill-out form. Help the person. Make it a social event. Do it with all children in attendance. 2. Make a tape recording during a quiet afternoon chat where you have an agenda to discuss specifics.

3. Make a home movie. Keep it light, and have fun using humor. *Vickie Kearney, MA, LPC*

When faced with the loss of its last living parent, my husband's family of six siblings excluded their spouses from decision making meetings, and nobody suffered hurt feelings. It just wasn't personal. I was inspired by that pleasant-as-possible-under-the-circumstances experience (unfettered by the distractions of spouses). Before he died, I asked Dad if he would stipulate that only his children be involved in any and all post-death decisions. Although he agreed it would be a good idea, there was no evidence he put it in writing.

What **W**ill Happen?

- **A Will.** This is one area where **most people need professional help** from a lawyer or an estate planner— **some kind of expert.**

- Trust **a Will** or trust a **trust**? A Will calls for the distribution of assets in a lump sum, as *pronto* as legally possible, upon death. A trust may call for the holding of assets for a period of time for gradual distribution until the trust is depleted.

- If a person writes down his wishes, but not necessarily in a Will, does that hold up legally? This is known as a **holographic Will,** and it can be considered valid, provided it is in the person's handwriting and the person signs it.

- **Possible problems with handwritten wishes** include that if someone claims a deceased person's holographic Will is valid, that someone has the burden of establishing that the deceased person did write it and was of sound mind at the time.

- Courts can be **reluctant to recognize holographic Wills** if the decedent's intent is uncertain, the writing is not clear, or the draft is not signed or effectively witnessed.

- **The Living Will.** It is an official, written health care declaration that clearly documents your wishes concerning medical treatment in the event you are not able to communicate. It is a good thing to have, just in case. Suggested web search words are: "**advance directives.**"

eXecutor/eXecutriX

Where There's A Will, There's A . . . Search.

EVEN THOUGH SHE was not the first born, my sister, Julie, was the executrix of Dad's estate. This made sense. She lived closest to him.

> **Estate Planning Tip:**
>
> Executor ("Executrix," if female), personal representative (PR), and administrator are all similar terms.
> *John N. McNamara, Jr.,*
> *Denver Attorney*

But none of us could locate the Will on the afternoon he was buried. We knew we could always call Dad's lawyer and get another copy. Before that call was necessary, the Will turned up. Julie's husband produced it.

Reading Of The Will And Rifling Through The Wallet

WE ALL—SIBLINGS and spouses (despite my husband's cautionary asides to me that it would be a bad idea to include the spouses)—gathered around the table. Julie held the Will packet in front of her. She dumped out the contents, which included the Will and some small, folded pieces of paper. Julie unfolded one and an "oops" escaped her mouth before she stuffed all the little papers back in the envelope.

I asked, "What was that?"

No answer. I asked again. Again, no answer. But I figured it out.

Those little folded papers were debts owed to Dad from us kids, debts to be subtracted from a son or daughter's inheritance.

Julie read aloud from the document. The Will contained no surprises, but I was surprised that no one else asked to see what was written on the folded pieces of paper. They got tucked away in my sister's care.

> **✔ Legal Advice:**
>
> In some states, the executor is required to provide an inventory to the beneficiaries or file it with the probate court within a certain time period. If the executor never provides accountings and the administration continues on indefinitely, the beneficiaries could go to court to force the executor to produce the information.
> *John N. McNamara, Jr.,*
> *Denver Attorney*

We found insurance policies our parents had taken out on my brother and one of my sisters. Someone joked that Mom and Dad must not have loved the other two, the ones without policies.

Jo's Coping Technique:
Denial. Elderly people have sexual urges, too. Just not my parent.

When Julie pulled out Dad's wallet and thumbed through it, a "coupon" fell out. It was handwritten by Dad's girlfriend, Ellie, "good for two nights at the motel of your choice." Hoots and hollers ensued.

What I Have Learned From My "X"s

- **An executor may be named in a Will or appointed by probate** if the executor is deceased or one has not been named in a Will. **Probate** is a court process whereby a deceased person's property is divided and distributed according to a Will. If there is no Will, property is divided and distributed by state laws on intestate succession. (*Intestate* means no Will was made before death, and *succession* means a series of things following each other in order—something a lawyer told me about and had to explain twice.)
- **Probate court?** That can be ugly. Let's not go there.
- **The role of the executor** is to make sure the wishes of the deceased are carried out as much as possible. The executor is responsible for delivering the estate plan documents to the attorney, who will probate the estate.
- **If the Will is contested,** the executor may be required to show up in court.

- **More than one executor can be named.** In some families, all surviving children are named as co-executors, and votes are taken for decision making.
- Naming a **non-family member as the executor** of your Will might be a good idea, depending on the relationship dynamics of your survivors.
- **Advice from two who've been there, done that executor thing:**
  - ✓ Baby Boomer Mary, who's had the job more than once, says, "**Find a knowledgeable, prompt, and fair attorney—** one who keeps you focused when emotions are high. It takes a lot of time, and you can charge the estate a reasonable amount to do this work. It's important that the executor **'play nice.'** Even if there is someone included in the estate you don't think should be, **it is not your estate,** and the courts mandate that you **execute it according to the Will.** The anxiety and potential litigation cost far more in the long run. Do the right thing knowing you have no personal liability, or at least, knowing you can defend your personal liability should a feud erupt."
  - ✓ Baby Boomer Gary B. says, "I was the executor of my mother's estate. Dealing with that responsibility on top of my grief was one of the hardest things I've ever done. Thankfully, Mom was organized. I can't imagine how I would have survived if I had been handling the affairs of someone with less foresight. My **advice for anyone who will have an executor is to write down some specifics**, not a Last Will And Testament, but other elements that could

assist the loved one who will have to deal with the details of your life—from where your bank accounts and safe-deposit boxes are located, to requests for music to be played at what kind of a service. **Put it in an envelope marked 'To be opened upon my death',** and make sure someone knows where it is. It's a huge, priceless gift."

Yard Sales Versus Estate Sales

Take The Yard Sales, Please

YARD SALES. RUTHIE loved going to them, and she loved having them. I helped Ruth with a yard sale—only once. It was more like a "showing" of garage sale items. We hauled all the junk out of her garage and arranged it invitingly on the driveway. I listened and watched for an entire Saturday during which Ruthie refused to bargain with shoppers.

"Lady, will you take $5 for this bird cage?"

The lady's response was, "My dear man, that is a one-of-a-kind, *wrought-iron* bird cage purchased from a highly respected and lovely antiques store on Broadway. For years it has graced my PAH-tee-oh (her preferred way of pronouncing *patio*) and provided whimsical delight for many a luncheon guest. The dried flower arrangement inside the cage *alone* is worth more than the money you offer. I cannot accept a penny less than $35."

When I heard her say that, I almost choked on my cream cheese Danish.

If anyone questioned her high prices, Ruth became insulted and delivered a verbal assault. At the end of the day, after nothing had sold, we hauled the junk back into her garage where it stayed until the next sale—or, rather, "showing."

Repeatedly, I told Ruthie that I would not help her with another one of her so-called yard sales because it didn't even resemble a yard sale. It was a "reconfiguration of discards on pavement" and an embarrassment.

Do-It-Yourself, Pre-Death?

A GROUP OF ladies pitched their estate sale company wanting to set up shop in Ruthie's house before she died. She gave them a day-long, elaborate tour of her beautiful things and abruptly dismissed them when she learned they were not bonded.

 Estate Sale Tip:

When enlisting the services of an estate sale company, find out about its reputation. Ask for references and contact them. Check the company's status with the Better Business Bureau.
Lisa Lee, Estate Sale Company Owner

"What if I held my own estate sale?" Ruthie wondered aloud. Did *I* know any cops she could hire to provide security? Would my sons, "Darling Beau" and "That Jack," help out? Would I help out? We decided it was too much for us to handle. Plus, I was still stinging from the yard sale experience with Ruthie from years earlier.

While a grand estate sale might have been what Ruthie envisioned in her home after she "tiptoed away," an estate liquidator was actually given the job of selling her massive amounts of worldly possessions.

 Estate Sale Tip:

Estate Liquidators are not known for sales. They conduct auctions of consolidated items from more than one estate. Items are grouped in categories (like furniture, art, statuary) and sold to the highest bidders.

*Lisa Lee, Estate Sale Company Own*er

More On Yard Sales ("moron yard sales?") And Estate Sales

- For safety's sake, hire security or entice some men to hang around the **yard sale** of an elderly woman. **Don't let strangers know this person lives alone.**
- **Be open to negotiation.** Otherwise you will be dragging everything back inside at the end of the day.
- You can **hold your own estate sale.** It's called *a living-estate sale.*
- The **definition** of "estate" is everything you own, all of your assets (whether real property or personal property) and liabilities.
- "By the time an estate sale company enters the picture," *Lisa Lee of Bye Gones Estate Sale*s says, "the family or friends have already gone through everything and taken what they want—although it does happen that even after everything is set up and merchandised for the sale, **the family or friends sneak in** when we aren't there and 'remove' (steal) additional items. It's now in my company's contract that my company is entitled to its commission on everything, including items that might have been removed, once sale set-up has begun."

Zzzzzzzz

Sleepover

A ROUGH DAY for Ruthie. I got her comfy. She gave herself a dropper of the heavy stuff and zonked out until dusk. When her eyes fluttered open and she asked me what I was still doing there, I told her I was spending the night.

"Why?"

Keeping it light, I told her, "I wanna know what happens here at night."

She seemed happy enough about that. When her son, David, called later, he did not seem to know what to make of it because he asked me, "What are you doing at my mother's house so late?"

Out of Ruth's earshot, I told him how she'd had a rough day, and I wanted to see how things might go during the night for her.

He seemed appreciative. "I know you're close to my mother, and she considers you to be somewhat like a daughter. For a long time, I was jealous of your relationship with her, but I'm not anymore. I'm glad you're there for her."

"Thanks for saying that."

> ## Expert Interpretation:
>
> As people begin to cross over, they connect to the other side. During the transition they might see spirit guides, loved ones, or angels. For most, it is welcoming and comforting. They feel as if they are going home. If they haven't connected with parents, other family members, and friends in years, they are likely to feel their presence as well.
> *Deb Sheppard,*
> *Medium and Intuitive Counselor*

It was a long night. Ruth talked and laughed in her sleep. She must have attended a party in her dreams, because she congenially addressed several people, calling them by names I didn't know. Names from her past, perhaps?

In the wee hours, she got up. Feigning sleep, I monitored her through half-shut eyes as Ruthie lit a cigarette and stood while she puffed, propped by one hand braced on the night stand. After stubbing out her cigarette, she got back in bed and "dreamchatted" again. Bella hopped on the bed and curled up next to me. It was too crowded and noisy for sleep. I waited for the sunrise and then got out of bed.

The Final Dance

A FEW NIGHTS later, I could not convince Ruth to get ready for bed. Her ankles and feet were swollen. She got up from the table and hobbled around the kitchen.

The dog came in with muddy paws. I dipped Bella's feet in a bowl of warm water, and as I wiped them dry, I sang *The Hokey Pokey*.

"You put your front paw in. You take your front paw out. You put your . . ."

Ruth joined in and took over the song, ". . . and you shake it all about. Then you do the Hokey Pokey, and you turn yourself around. That's what it's all about."

With her back to me, she was singing at the top of her lungs, moving her hips like a saloon girl, dancing as best she could on those swollen, stumpy legs and feet. (Should I laugh or cry?)

Ruth shuffled around her kitchen, scanning and perusing. It was as if she knew she was seeing her beautiful things for the last time. She drank it all in.

Sleepover Number Two

FOR THE FIRST time, Ruthie didn't try to throw me off her side as I helped her up the stairs, for what would be the last time. We got her ready for bed. And then I told her I was spending the night.

"Why? I'm fine."

"I know."

I didn't tell her it was because I wanted to introduce her to the caregiver, who would be there the next morning to begin round-the-clock care, and who had been hired behind her back. No way would she would be happy about that. At least I should be there to face the music.

For this sleepover, I pulled the mattress off the sleeper sofa in the room across the hall and positioned it on the floor so I could see her during the night. I let Bella outside. By the time the dog and I returned, Ruth was asleep, and the show began.

Bella curled up next to me on the mattress and snoozed while her owner called out in the night. Ruth was calling out for . . . someone. The words were jumbled. Her sleep was fitful. At times she reached her arms out into the air as if trying to grasp someone or something. She had a look of intense concentration on her face.

Wake Up And Smell The Coffee

MY OWN SLEEP was fitful as well, so I got up early, went downstairs, and waited anxiously for the agency caregiver to arrive. Ruth was still sleeping when the woman arrived, but Bella's barking and the cowbells hanging on the front door woke her, and she called out, "Who's there?"

"Just me," I called back. "I'll be up in a minute."

The hired caregiver needed to be debriefed.

"She'll resist you being here. I don't know what's going to happen," I told her.

The caregiver gave me a knowing look as if she'd been through this sort of thing before.

We climbed the stairs together, Bella underfoot with a "fluffy" in her mouth. I wondered how the dog could treat this so lightly. Her owner was going to flip out.

"Ruthie, this is Rose. She's here to help take care of you." Gulp. Silence.

"Hi, Rose." A cordial enough response, but she knew what was going on and shot me a dagger look.

"Ruthie, your trustee told me to hire a caregiving service. Please don't be upset."

Rose took over, engaged Ruth in some light conversation, and put her at ease. They instantly got along swimmingly. Rose was getting Ruth up and ready for the day, so I kissed Ruthie and headed for my car.

Then I remembered the money.

Sock The Money Away

I WENT BACK into the house, amidst the clamor of the cowbells on the front door and dog yaps, and called out, "It's just me. I forgot something."

"Okay, darling girl," Ruthie shouted from upstairs. She was busy being attended to.

With Bella on my heels, and hungry for attention, I hurried up into Ruth's "Go-To-Hell" room (her messy office/guest room), grabbed the money bag, and turned. But Bella's whining made me pause. I sat down so she could jump in my lap. I took a pen and wrote *call your trustee* on a piece of paper, slipped it in the bag, and pulled out the money. Bella jumped down.

I stuffed a few thousand dollars into my pocket and yelled, "See you later, Ruth."

I didn't think that Rose or any other caregiver would steal from Ruthie. I just thought that Ruthie might *worry* about the caregiver stealing from her. If she happened to check on her cash stash, which she often did, and found it gone, that little note in its place would go a long way to ease her mind.

All that money stuffed in my pocket made me paranoid. What if someone rammed me in my car

Home Health Care Tip:

Reputable agencies hire bonded, insured and formally trained caregivers, but many work independently. Clients sometimes hire independent caregivers because it's more affordable, but there could be serious risks involved.
Audrey DiGiorgio, Administrator,
Continued Care Retirement Community

and stole the money at gunpoint? On the way home, I called Ruth's trustee on my cell phone and asked him if I should bring the money over. He told me to keep it at my house for the time being. He would get it later.

I stashed Ruthie's mad money in my husband's sock drawer.

The Changing Of The Guard

MARIE SAID SHE would introduce Ruthie's next caregiver at the shift change. It worked. Another smooth transition, so we assumed that Ruthie was fine with this new arrangement. Wrong.

The next morning at seven, a new caregiver took over for the all-night caregiver. My name was at the top of the phone tree, so I got the call.

"Uh, hello. I'm from the agency, and Miss Ruthie wants to speak to you."

The receiver noisily changed hands. Ruthie growled into the phone, "That's a dirty, rotten trick you played on me."

Home Health Care Tip:

Hired caregivers are not allowed to speak on behalf of the patient or talk to others about the patient (unless it's to another caregiver from the same agency and pertains to the job). It's against the rules to give out information to anyone but the patient or someone legally named as a representative of the patient. If the patient has signed a HIPAA release, specific information can be shared with specific people named in the release.
Audrey DiGiorgio, Administrator,
Continued Care Retirement Community

"I'll be right there."

As fast as I could get there, I got there. I kicked myself the entire way for not being there for the caregiver shift change. I had let Ruthie down. She trusted me, and I had deceived her. It was because of me that she was confused, afraid, and uncomfortable in her own home.

As I climbed the stairs, guilt consumed me. My head hung low as I turned the corner and walked into her bedroom. I braced for the worst.

"Hello, darling girl. What are you doing here?"

The agency caregiver was fluffing the pillows, getting Ruth comfy in her bed.

Before I could answer, she drifted off to sleep. She never entirely woke up again.

The Last Days

A DREAMLIKE STATE took over. There were times when Ruth opened her eyes, locked them with mine, and smiled. Other times, she furrowed her brow and moved her mouth as if talking with someone in serious conversation. Of course, the worst times were when she winced with pain, so I sang hymns. Hymns soothed Ruthie. After the first few notes, her eyebrows lifted, and she moved her lips with the lyrics. Her eyes stayed shut. Sometimes, the group of us friends sang to her. It was

Expert Interpretation:

Those who are in the process of transition do hear us—our words, our music—and feel our touch. The body shuts down but not the soul. The soul can experience the transition by practicing being in both realms. This happens mostly with those who are ill for a period of time and are preparing for their passing.
Deb Sheppard,
Medium and Intuitive Counselor

Home Health Care Tip:

Unless they are nurses, caregivers from hired agencies can't dispense drugs. They can only hand them to the patient, and the patient has to give herself the medication.
Audrey DiGiorgio, Administrator,
Continued Care Retirement Community

hardly a choir of angels, but we hoped it sounded sweet enough to ease her mind.

People came over for last visits. Her trustee brought flowers, sat by her bedside, and held her hand.

Friends and nurses, Colonel Betty and Marie, filled droppers with morphine so the caregivers could hand them to Ruthie as needed.

By day, Ruth's friends were there. Her son was there in the evenings and at night. The hospice nurse made house calls and suggested we give Ruthie permission to go.

After a few days, a joint decision was made to move Ruth downstairs. This was a difficult decision because, in the earlier stages of her illness, Ruth had resisted having a hospital bed in her home and maintained she wanted to die in her own bed on the second floor. But a baby monitor was not cutting it anymore. Ruth needed to be in the family room, near the laundry facilities, kitchen, bathroom, and caregiver.

The hospice delivered a hospital bed and told us to call the fire department to move her downstairs. Huh? Call the fire department? We could not believe we could just call the fire department and they would pop on over for this, but we called the fire department, anyway, and they said they would be over in ten minutes.

"Can you give us fifteen?"

It seemed impossible that they would actually come *right* over, so we were not actually ready. They pulled up in exactly fifteen minutes. Four firefighters—two men and two women—showed up in full

Expert Interpretation:

I've had several opportunities to connect with someone who hasn't made the transition to the other side and feels blocked, perhaps from fear. Hospice nurses and family have asked to give the person a feeling of safety and permission to release themselves from this earthly connection. Within minutes, they allow themselves this freedom. It is remarkable for the family to see the peace that takes place.
Deb Sheppard,
Medium and Intuitive Counselor

regalia and tromped behind us up the stairs. Ruthie seemed unaware that they were in the room, until they touched her. Although they handled her, as if she was their own mother, when they transferred her—sheets, pillows, and all—onto a backboard, the sensation upset her and she cried out, "No, no, no . . . "

One firefighter saw me choke back a tear. She caught my eye and said, "She's all right."

They gently carried our friend to the makeshift medical center downstairs and set her on the bed. We asked if there was payment due, and one said, "No ma'am. This is part of our job."

As they rode off in their big red truck they waved goodbye, and Marie said she would send a thank-you note.

We pulled chairs over to one side of the bed, stroked Ruthie's hair, and held her hand in hopes she would adjust to the new surroundings. Bella gingerly jumped up on the bed and licked her owner's other hand. The caregiver began the cycle of laundry, changing the bed, and keeping a journal.

First Responders:

Tips are not accepted, but cards or letters are greatly appreciated, especially the ones sent to supervisors.
Mike Osgood, Engineer/Firefighter

All that was left to do? Wait for Ruthie to "tiptoe away."

Remembering the suggestion of the hospice nurse, I whispered to my friend, "Ruthie, you're good to go."

Sweet DreamZzzzzz

"How do you want to die?" Most people say they would prefer to die in their sleep. Get ready for bed, kiss your sweetheart goodnight, and never wake up.

Jo's Glossary

Terms I didn't know or wasn't sure about until I wrote this book

bone picker - someone who makes off with a deceased person's possessions as soon as death occurs. Also known as a vulture.

cremains - death industry combo buzzword for "cremated remains."

decedent - a dead person. Coroners use this word a lot.

grave spinning - what a decedent might be doing ("spinning in his grave") if his or her dying wishes are not carried out or respected.

greed goggles - like "beer goggles," only you're under the influence of a strong desire for *money* and *stuff* instead of alcohol. Example: When a person borrows a backhoe and churns up a decedent's yard in search of buried treasure— I didn't make that up—the greed goggles are on.

grief-guilt or grief buying - picking out and buying an extravagant, expensive casket for Mom because you feel guilty about something you did or said to her when you were 18. And later you think the funeral director took advantage of you.

non-titled property - personal property not named in the Will. The stuff over which family squabbles are made.

palliative - care that relieves pain and controls symptoms without curing. A comfort word.

surface swimmer - what a therapist might call someone who won't dive deeper for a better understanding. A surface swimmer only skims along the top of the water, which still makes for that "rippling" effect.

testator - a fancy word for a man who has made out a Will. Lawyers and courts use this word.

testatrix - an even fancier word for a woman who has made out a Will. I have never heard anyone else actually use this word, maybe because it sounds kinky when you say it. (Say it. See what I mean?)

thanatologist - highbrow word for grief counselor. You sound smart when you say that word.

Afterword From The Afterworld

Joanne,

Nobody's more surprised than me that I died.

I lived through working in a coal mine, WWII, multiple by-pass surgeries, falling off a scaffolding, a hurricane, and getting run over by my own truck. Who'd have thought I'd trip and hit my head while shooting pool, and that would be the way I'd go?

Life's funny like that. Death's funny like that, I guess. It's not funny, though, how you kids are not close to each other since your momma and I passed away. I want each of you to pick out a switch and give yourself a pants-down whipping.

Ya'll know I'm not very good at expressing my feelings. It makes me cry to talk about serious stuff. You kids should talk. WE should have talked. After your mother died, I wish I had sat down with the four of you. And I should have called a meeting after the truck accident. If I'd had a plan, things would be different. But, that's how it goes. You don't get a do-over.

Well, I miss you. Make an effort to get along, now, and be a happy family. I can't speak for your mother, but she's probably also spinning in her grave . . . right next to mine.

Love,
Dad

P.S. Jo, I know you bought it for me, but I want your brother to have the remote-controlled fart machine. He'll have as much fun with it as I did.

Acknowledgments

Good to Go could never have been written without the professionals who generously offered tips and those who have survived the passing of their elders. I am forever grateful to you all for sharing your valuable time, expertise, and experiences for this book for the sake of helping others.

Good to Go would never have been completed without friends and family. Thank you all.

John, Beau, and Jack for encouraging me to follow my dreams.

Melanie Mulhall, my editor, and Nick Zelinger, my designer, for crawling up inside my head and holding my hand. Paula Kinnes, for the final edit, thanks a gazillion.

Deborah Ferris and Melissa Hubka Swedlund, true professionals in the death care industry who really do care. How wonderful that people like you are there to provide the comfort with the service.

Tom Hoch. No matter where in the world you happen to be, you are there for me with tech support and a wry comment that keeps me grounded.

Greg Martin, who never considers himself too busy—or a time of day too inconvenient—to help a friend with an IT need. Ann Martin and James Martin, thanks for graciously lending me the man of your house.

Jenna, Kara, Molly, and Catie for your proficiencies in clerical organization, transcription, manuscript reproduction, and computer technology. You are lovely little *Good to Go-fers.*

John Horan, for giving me valuable time and information. You are a gem.

Cousin Buddy, for sharing the memories of your youth and for providing a cherished connection to the grandfather I never knew.

Wayne bo, Jared, Joyce, Theresa, Barb, Al and Rebecca, Maria, Glenn, Reverend Karen, Gov and Biz, Susie, Roger and Garnette, Doyle, Evelinda and Judie, Laurel, Ted, Debra, Diane, Frank, and Ali for your help and encouragement.

"The Girls," my chosen sisters: Jeri Jo, Ruth Ann, Pamela Sue, and Kathy Marie.

"The Ladies," my adopted moms: Gloria, Adeline, Eileen, and Colonel Margaret. And, Colonel Margaret, a special thanks to you for sharing your amazing exit plans. Of anyone I know, you are the most good to go.

Why Jo Wrote This Book

FUELED BY MY experiences and a longtime interest in the lives and times of the generation before me, *Good to Go* virtually wrote itself.

Perhaps because I never knew my grandparents, I have always been curious about elderly people, felt they have much to offer, and lamented when I have witnessed them ignored or disrespected.

Most memories are lovely.

As a member of a volunteer group assigned to visit nursing homes, I have enjoyed the company of countless aged people—some forgotten or without family—heard their stories, and observed the care they received.

The popular music of my parents' generation was adopted by my band, *Jo Myers and The Mama's Boys*. We performed our own special brand of standards from the 1930s and 1940s. Our audiences of seniors did not seem to mind when I perverted lyrics or sang *My Buddy* in pig latin. They sang along, applauded, and laughed enthusiastically.

An elderly cousin once took me on a "granny-tracking" jaunt to meet newly discovered, distant elderly relatives who carried stories from the Civil War era about the ancestors buried on their property. The experience was unforgettable. (This daytrip ended with a recap over a shared plate of greasy-spoon onion rings—my cousin's favorite food—which also stayed with me for a very long time.)

And I love the exploration of a cemetery, traipsing around with my camera and snapping pictures of statues, headstones, and old trees.

I have toured graveyards in places as far away as Sweden, Slovenia, and Mexico, but it was in the one closest to home that I gave my son an impromptu math lesson. Pointing to headstones, I asked him, "Beau, how old was this guy when he died? How old was this person when she died?" (It was a fun game until he realized he was learning subtraction!)

While I am certainly not the perfect mother, daughter, sister, wife, or friend, I feel strongly that a family unit should remain intact, especially after a death. However, sometimes "should" simply does not happen. "Should" has a better chance if a plan is in place.

Now, who is good to go?

A Chance To Contribute Your Stories!

While writing *Good to Go*, I discovered that many friends and acquaintances were interested in the topic. Reaction ranged from commiseration, "Oh, you should hear what happened when *my* parents died . . . ," to concern, "My family should talk. . . before it's too late."

One woman confided that she hired a lawyer when her husband died, so she could protect herself from her adult stepchildren.

A man, inspired by my project, convinced his mother to hold a family meeting, politely excluding the spouses of her adult children.

After hearing about my book, an aging widow was prompted to list the family heirlooms and attach a child's name to each for fair and equal distribution of property upon her death.

If you have a personal story about your own experience with an aspect of death and dying covered in this book and would like to contribute it for a *Good to Go* sequel, **I would love to hear from you.** Please visit the web address listed below and e-mail me your stories. Include your name, address, e-mail address, and a statement allowing the release of your story(ies) in print and/or electronic sequels to this book.

Thank you.
Jo Myers
www.goodtogothebook.com

Book Jo For Your Event

A thirty-year veteran of major market radio in Denver, Atlanta, South Florida, Cincinnati, and Nashville, Jo Myers is a seasoned professional speaker who offers an entertaining and thought-provoking approach to death and dying.

To book her for your next event or for more information about Jo's keynote talks, visit **www.goodtogothebook.com.**

To Order Additional Copies of
Good to Go

go to www.goodtogothebook.com